Why Add Water When Wine Will Do

Memories of Recipes and Food's Pleasures

Heidi Smith

Copyright © 2014 by Heidi M Smith
All rights reserved. No parts of this book may be reproduced
or retransmitted in any form or by any means without the
written permission of the publisher.

Trade Paperback Edition

Also by Heidi Smith
After The Bombs – My Berlin
Memoir

**Forks in the Road -
My New Life In America**
Memoir

Orchard Books
PO Box 1819
Taos, New Mexico 87571
www.HeidiSmithGroup.com

ISBN 978-0-578-15353-7

To Trent, Jason, Shakti and Derek,
the most appreciative gourmands and gourmets I know.

*"There is no love sincerer
than the love of food."*

George Bernard Shaw

Contents

Welcome To My Kitchen	1
This'n That Before You Start	3
About Wines	4
Starters	6
Soups & Sauces	19
Breads & Crepes	34
Pizza & Pasta	48
Salads	57
Vegetables & Sides	63
The Good Egg	93
Gifts From The Sea	100
Things With Wings	105
All About Beef	117
Lamb	134
Pork & Veal	143
Wild Things	152
Finales	161
Edible Flowers	186
Index	187
Essential Tools	190
Most Dog-Eared Cookbooks	192

Welcome to My Kitchen

I'm addicted to cooking, and I know there's no cure for me.

    I fully blame my mother for this addiction. Doesn't everybody blame their mother for something? If she hadn't been such a purist about fresh ingredients, I might be happy just heating up a TV dinner. If she hadn't debated with herself in front of me, "Should I boil these onions, or would they taste better sautéed?" I wouldn't have spent a fortune on cookbooks.

    If her cooking hadn't created delectable aromas wafting through our Berlin apartment, I might be content having dinner in restaurants four to five times a week, like many people do. But what fun is that? I'd rather cook for three hours and anticipate the meal the entire time.

    When I was eighteen, serendipity sent an opportunity my way to work as cook in Switzerland and I accepted. Until then, brewing coffee and sandwich making was the sum of my cooking experience. But I had observed my mother's skills in the kitchen while growing up in Germany for years.

    As a cooking apprentice, I felt at home in that Swiss kitchen right away. After six weeks of "kitchen boot camp" – that's how I perceived the apprenticeship - I presented a formal five-course dinner. It was a success. I was hooked.

    A day without cooking is a dark one to me, whether the sun is shining or not. When I go on vacation for more than a couple of days, a kitchen has to be accessible. Most people would rejoice when told, "Oh, you don't have to cook!" To me that would be purgatory.

    Since 1960 I've cooked continually. That makes over 20,000 meals if I count only one meal per day. I've been a personal chef; I've headed the kitchen at an exclusive ski club; I've been a chef for retreats and I've been a caterer. For a while I was even a cook-off junkie, traveling all over the U.S and meeting similar addicts.

My introduction to cooking was based on classic French cuisine. Since then I've learned and experimented on my own. Wine has been ever present in my kitchen. When I realized that alcohol evaporates during cooking, "Why add water when wine will do?" became my mantra. It also gave me permission to use a recipe as *inspiration,* not as an iron-clad how-to.

Always budget minded, I've simplified recipes, adapting them for everyday use. Such recipes have worked just as well in more formal settings and when serving a crowd.

But nothing has been more satisfying to me than cooking for my family. From the time my three children were small, they wanted to take turns at the stove. They demonstrated that cooking can be child's play indeed. When he was five, Derek insisted, "I wanna bake a chicken like you do." Shakti was seven when she declared, "I'm making Spanish Rice for show and tell." Jason was eleven when I arrived home from the store to find him waiting in the kitchen wearing a big grin. "I have a surprise," he said, "You'll never guess!" I tried to guess but couldn't figure out what he'd been up to. Jason quickly opened a cabinet door, "Ta – Da!" and pulled out a platter with freshly made cream puffs – my absolute favorite (next to chocolate).

When I call my grown children today, more times than not I catch them in the kitchen. They might be making tortellini, baking bread or creating a fancy dessert for their families. Jason, Shakti and Derek may not realize it yet, but they too are hopelessly addicted.

My husband Trent was, and is, happy to taste anything coming out of our kitchen. Over the years he has embraced cooking also. Baking is his specialty.

This cookbook is a collection of often-requested recipes and personal favorites. Well known German standards are included; some are Berlin specialties. French and Italian country cooking is represented, as well as examples of my forays into international cuisine. Since moving to the Southwest, Chile peppers have been sneaking into stews and other dishes.

I'm hoping this book will feed your cooking addiction too.

Heidi Smith

Taos, New Mexico
2014

This'n That Before You Start

Over the past fifty years we've gone from cooking from scratch, to pre-packaged everything, to public awareness of the value of cooking with the best ingredients we can find again. Here are my latest suggestions:

1: Except for olive oil, I've replaced all oils with non-hydrogenated ones. Non-hydrogenated is the only kind of fat/oil to use, whatever type you prefer. All others have been processed and are detrimental to everyone's health. I use extra-virgin cold pressed coconut oil; it does not impart any flavor and performs well under high temperatures. As with eggs, coconut oil has been accused of causing high cholesterol, but slowly and especially more recently, information to the contrary has emerged. Do investigate on your own. Hydrogenation is the culprit, and is widely used. Check labels – it is everywhere.

2: I use olive oil only when high heat temperatures are not required, and I love it for dipping and salad dressings.

3: Unsalted, organic butter is the other fat I use.

4: I have cut back on sugar and often replace it with honey, Agave or maple syrup, which are natural sweeteners, more easily absorbed and digested. In some deserts I still use sugar, although in reduced amounts, for best results.

5: It is not wise to cut salt out completely. The body needs sodium in minute amounts. It only takes a small amount of salt to bring out flavor in fresh foods, especially vegetables. I use unrefined sea salt because it is lower in sodium and contains minerals that are out-processed in commercial salt.

6: I have increased the amounts of garlic, herbs, and spices in all recipes. Herbs and spices contain antioxidants and are rich in minerals and vitamins. Many were used in medicinal treatments centuries ago.

7: In off-seasons I do buy canned organic tomatoes and some frozen vegetables. They are often a better option than the tired-looking and travel-weary produce available.

8: I avoid cheese toppings. Cheese tends to cover up other interesting flavors and adds fat and calories.

9: Cooking is not an exact science. Unless it is burned beyond recognition, if something turns out differently than expected, think of it as a new creation! Countless professionals have done just that.

About Wines

Wine has been ever present in my kitchen since Trent and I married. When we met, Trent and his brother Eric had a restaurant and bar, *The Inside Edge,* at the Sugarbush Ski Resort in Vermont. Trent was in charge of the dining room and wine service.

When we bought our home on a hillside in nearby Moretown in 1968, I raised vegetables. Trent raised sheep and grew grapes. The search for cold climate hardy varieties brought him to the agriculture department at Cornell University in New York. On their recommendation Trent planted Marechal Foch and immersed himself in viticulture.

We sought out reasonably priced wines continually to have a steady supply at home. Our stocked wine cellar allowed me to follow my whim, "Why add water when wine will do?" I experimented regularly to see how wine affected the final taste and was often delighted with the results. Wine brought depth of flavor, especially to meat dishes. I learned not to boil dishes when wine was added or the flavor would be lost.

When I know we will open a special bottle of wine at dinnertime, I do not use the same wine in my cooking. My common sense and natural thriftiness do not allow it. I use the same type of grape in a good drinkable, everyday jug wine instead.

In the mid 1970s Trent was looking forward to his first batch of red wine when we heard of an organic winery in southern Vermont. We were excited and visited. I had my first taste of an organic wine. It was awful, vinegar tasted better. I suspect it was not the "organic" part's fault.

Years later, in 1987, Trent and I visited the Parducci winery in Mendocino, California. John Parducci had maintained organic practices in his vineyards. But he didn't apply for the "organic" status because it is time consuming and expensive. During a long luncheon with John we tasted his whites and reds. Organic turned out to be delightful.

Other U.S. wineries also practiced sustainable methods – also referred to as biodynamic - at the time, Fetzer Winery in California, being one. Beringer, Frey, Krug, Mondavi, Phelps and Sutter were others and, like Parducci, are still going strong.

Organic and sustainable farming methods have been practiced by vintners for years. Under sustainable or biodynamic farming, crops are treated without chemicals and growers strive for the farm's ecosystem to be balanced, self-sustaining and healing.

Organic, biodynamic or sustainable labels are available in a wide variety of wines grown in the United States and many foreign countries as well. Gruet, Black Mesa and Vivac Wineries in New Mexico use organic and sustainable methods.

Trent had many good grape harvests and made an excellent dry red wine. He also made a special dry apple wine from heirloom apples in our orchard. It resembled a German Gewürztraminer, his favorite white wine.

I recommend experimenting with organic or sustainable wines for drinking and cooking as much as possible. But taste should be your main guide.

Prosit!

Starters

Artichoke Appetizer	7
Chicken Liver Pate	8
Deviled Eggs	9
Escargot	10
Garlic Butter	10
Guacamole	11
Puerto Angel Salsa	11
Herbed Puff Pastry Rings	12
Lamb in a Blanket	13
Pot Stickers	14
Raw Snacks	15
Steak Tartar	16
Steamed Mussels	17
Stuffed Mushrooms	18

In our family a formal first course was reserved for company. Informally, on a daily basis, we met before dinner to review the day's events. While nibbling on some Cabot cheddar cheese and crackers, everyone, including the children, had a turn to talk about what was most important. Especially during junior high and high school days, these gatherings helped air upsetting issues. Dinners were more relaxed this way.

One of the simplest appetizers is rolled nasturtium leaves stuffed with goat cheese. No need for a recipe. When the garden is in full bloom, this is the perfect starter.

Classic melon-wrapped prosciutto is simple, and hard to beat. It is worth waiting for a vine-ripened melon to create that perfect sweet and savory taste.

Artichoke Appetizer
A hands-on appetizer, not for the buffet table.

4 artichokes
Water
4 whole allspice
4 whole cloves
10 peppercorns
1 garlic clove, crushed
1 small onion, cut into quarters
1 bay leaf
⅛ teaspoon salt
½ cup mayonnaise
Reserved liquid
1 teaspoon fresh parsley, minced

Buy artichokes with leaves that are tightly closed.
Cut off tips of every leaf and all but 1-inch of the bottom stem.
Add enough water to submerge the artichokes, allspice, cloves, peppercorns, garlic, onion, bay leaf and salt to a large pot. Bring to a boil, lower heat, cover and simmer until artichokes are done, about 30 minutes. Test the bottom of the stem with a knife for tenderness.
Remove artichokes. Place artichokes upside down in a sieve, to let liquid drain, and cover to keep warm.
Thin mayonnaise, with some of the strained cooking liquid, to make a heavy cream-like dipping sauce. Add the parsley and serve in individual dishes.*
Place one artichoke and a dish with dipping sauce on a plate for each person.
4 servings
Eating: Put a bowl for the discarded leaves in the center of the table. Start pulling leaves off artichoke and dip the thick end lightly into the sauce. Scrape the bit of artichoke flesh off with your teeth. Discard leaves. Finally, at the fuzz near the bottom, slide a sharp knife between fuzz and the solid part below (the heart). Lift fuzz and discard.
Now the artichoke heart can be cut into pieces and dipped into the sauce.
(* A tangy vinaigrette can be served for dipping instead of the above.)

Creamy Chicken Liver Pate

An easy, do ahead crowd pleaser. Even vegetarians have been spotted to cross-over for a nibble. Leftovers will disappear quickly as sandwich spread.

¼ teaspoon freshly ground pepper
⅛ teaspoon allspice
1 pinch ground clove
⅛ teaspoon coriander
8 tablespoons unsalted butter
1 large onion, finely diced
1 pound chicken livers
Salt to taste
⅓ cup heavy cream or sour cream
1 tablespoons brandy*
2 teaspoons coarsely ground peppercorns** (optional)

Combine the first four spices, set aside.
If needed, cut livers in half and remove any visible membrane.
Melt 2 tablespoons butter in as skillet over medium heat; when foam subsides, add onion and sauté until softened, about 5 to 7 minutes. Remove onions with a slotted spoon, set aside.
Turn up heat slightly, add livers to pan and sprinkle with salt; sauté livers on one side until they begin to brown, about 3 to 5 minutes, then flip them and brown the other side. Be sure to keep the heat relatively high so that the outside of livers sears and the inside stays pink.
Empty contents of the pan into a food processor with onions, remaining butter, cream, spices and brandy. Puree mixture until smooth; taste and adjust seasoning.**
Scrape pâté into a terrine or bowl, smooth top and refrigerate for 2 to 3 hours or overnight, until fully set.***
Serve pate with crackers or crostini.

*   Use additional brandy according to taste.
**   I blend 1 teaspoon of coarsely ground black peppercorns into the mixture after pureeing.
***   I sprinkle 1 teaspoon coarsely ground black peppercorns over the smoothed surface.

Deviled Eggs

Deviled eggs are universally loved. They are a welcome addition at pot lucks or buffets dinners. No matter what peoples' diet may be, watch the eggs disappear.

12 eggs
3 tablespoons mayonnaise
1 teaspoon mild mustard
Salt and freshly ground pepper to taste
1 lemon, juiced
Capers or chives for decoration

Place the eggs in a saucepan and cover them with at least 1-inch of water.
Just before the water reaches a full boil – tiny bubbles are starting to come to the surface - turn off the heat and wait 10 minutes. The eggs will be firm without grey around the yolk's edges when they are peeled.
Drain water from pot and refill with cold water several times, until eggs are totally cooled off.
Remove from water into a bowl and refrigerate if they are not processed shortly. Eggs peel best when done within the hour of cooling.
Peel eggs, cut in half horizontally and remove yolks to a mixing bowl.
Crush yolks with a fork, add mayonnaise, mustard, salt, pepper and lemon juice and blend. Taste before proceeding
Have a serving plate large enough to hold the eggs nearby. One half at a time, refill the hollow in each half with the mixture, making a slight mound. Make a design in the top with a fork and place on the plate. Top the egg mixture with either 2 or 3 small capers or sprinkle with finely sliced chives.
Store covered in the refrigerator until needed.

1 dozen/24 halves

Escargots in Garlic Butter

The first time I had escargots it turned out to be dinner. Friends and I stopped at a country inn outside Strasbourg in France. We settled at the bar and ordered a dozen snails each. After wiping the shells clean with plenty of bread, we ordered another dozen and a salad each. Voila, what a dinner!

For a special appetizer 6 snails per serving are the norm.

12 snail shells
12 snails
Garlic butter, see below, as needed

Put a snail into the shell and cover with butter. Place on an escargot dish. In lieu of a special dish crumble enough aluminum foil on a baking sheet to make room for 12 indents to hold the snails.
Preheat oven to 425°F.
Heat snails for 10 minutes or until butter has melted and starting to brown.
Serve immediately with sliced French or Italian bread.

2 servings – for more servings simply multiply the recipe

Snails can also be put in white mushroom caps. Brush the top of each cap lightly with oil. Place a snail in the center of bottom of the cap and cover generously with butter.
Line a baking sheet with parchment to hold mushroom caps.
Bake in 425°F oven for 10 minutes.

Garlic Butter

I always have a batch in the refrigerator. It is handy when making garlic bread, or even as a vegetable or meat topping.

8 tablespoons unsalted butter, softened
3 cloves garlic, minced fine
1 tablespoon fresh parsley, minced
1 teaspoon lemon juice
⅛ teaspoon freshly ground pepper

Mix all ingredients well in advance and keep in the refrigerator.

Deviled Eggs

Deviled eggs are universally loved. They are a welcome addition at pot lucks or buffets dinners. No matter what peoples' diet may be, watch the eggs disappear.

12 eggs
3 tablespoons mayonnaise
1 teaspoon mild mustard
Salt and freshly ground pepper to taste
1 lemon, juiced
Capers or chives for decoration

Place the eggs in a saucepan and cover them with at least 1-inch of water.
Just before the water reaches a full boil – tiny bubbles are starting to come to the surface - turn off the heat and wait 10 minutes. The eggs will be firm without grey around the yolk's edges when they are peeled.
Drain water from pot and refill with cold water several times, until eggs are totally cooled off.
Remove from water into a bowl and refrigerate if they are not processed shortly. Eggs peel best when done within the hour of cooling.
Peel eggs, cut in half horizontally and remove yolks to a mixing bowl.
Crush yolks with a fork, add mayonnaise, mustard, salt, pepper and lemon juice and blend. Taste before proceeding
Have a serving plate large enough to hold the eggs nearby. One half at a time, refill the hollow in each half with the mixture, making a slight mound. Make a design in the top with a fork and place on the plate. Top the egg mixture with either 2 or 3 small capers or sprinkle with finely sliced chives.
Store covered in the refrigerator until needed.

1 dozen/24 halves

Escargots in Garlic Butter

The first time I had escargots it turned out to be dinner. Friends and I stopped at a country inn outside Strasbourg in France. We settled at the bar and ordered a dozen snails each. After wiping the shells clean with plenty of bread, we ordered another dozen and a salad each. Voila, what a dinner!

For a special appetizer 6 snails per serving are the norm.

12 snail shells
12 snails
Garlic butter, see below, as needed

Put a snail into the shell and cover with butter. Place on an escargot dish. In lieu of a special dish crumble enough aluminum foil on a baking sheet to make room for 12 indents to hold the snails.
Preheat oven to 425°F.
Heat snails for 10 minutes or until butter has melted and starting to brown.
Serve immediately with sliced French or Italian bread.

2 servings – for more servings simply multiply the recipe

Snails can also be put in white mushroom caps. Brush the top of each cap lightly with oil. Place a snail in the center of bottom of the cap and cover generously with butter.
Line a baking sheet with parchment to hold mushroom caps.
Bake in 425°F oven for 10 minutes.

Garlic Butter

I always have a batch in the refrigerator. It is handy when making garlic bread, or even as a vegetable or meat topping.

8 tablespoons unsalted butter, softened
3 cloves garlic, minced fine
1 tablespoon fresh parsley, minced
1 teaspoon lemon juice
⅛ teaspoon freshly ground pepper

Mix all ingredients well in advance and keep in the refrigerator.

Best Guacamole
Everyone has their favorite 'Guac' recipe. This is mine.

3 ripe avocados
2 tomatoes, chopped
1 medium onion, minced
1 lime, juiced
Salt and pepper to taste

Cut avocados in half, scoop out the flesh and mash in a bowl until smooth.
Mix in all other ingredients.
Let it sit for at least 1 hour.

Taste and serve.

(Since we've moved to New Mexico, I occasionally add one finely chopped roasted green chile pepper for variety of flavor.)

Puerto Angel Salsa
This was served at a small beachfront palapa in Puerto Angel, on the Pacific coast of Mexico. Fresh, ripe ingredients make the best salsa.

10 tomatoes, diced
1 large yellow onion, chopped
3 cloves garlic, minced
Salt and pepper to taste
½ cup Cilantro, chopped

Mix all ingredients well. Let the salsa sit for 30 minutes.
Adjust seasonings and serve.

Herbed Puff Pastry Rings

Very easy to prepare ahead, keep in the refrigerator and bake when needed.

1 sheet puff pastry, thawed
1 cup fresh parsley, minced
½ cup fresh basil, minced
1 medium onion, grated or minced very fine
2 garlic cloves, minced
⅛ teaspoon salt
Freshly ground pepper
½ cup parmesan cheese, grated
¼ cup breadcrumbs
1 egg mixed with 1 tablespoon water

Preheat oven to 400°F. Line a rimmed baking sheet with foil.
Mix parsley, basil, garlic, salt, pepper, parmesan and breadcrumbs until thoroughly blended.
Unfold the pastry sheet onto a lightly floured surface. With a rolling pin work the pastry until it is 20-inches wide. Brush sheet with the egg mixture. Spread the herbs evenly over the pastry to within ½-inch of the edges.
Roll the wide side of the pastry into a tight roll. Cut the roll into ½-inch slices and put them cut-side down on the baking sheet, leaving about 1-inch space between each.
Bake for 15 minutes or until golden brown.
Serve hot.

40 servings

Lamb in a Blanket

An abundance of ground lamb, a residual effect of raising sheep, inspired this recipe

1 sheet puff pastry, thawed
1 pound ground lamb
½ cup bread crumbs
1 egg
1 large onion, finely minced
1 clove garlic, minced
1 teaspoon fresh rosemary, finely minced
¼ teaspoon each salt and pepper
Water as needed
1 egg mixed with a little water for brushing the pastry

Preheat oven to 350°F. Line a rimmed baking sheet with parchment paper.
Unfold puff pastry and roll out to roughly 9x16 on a lightly floured board. Cut the pastry in half lengthwise.
In a bowl mix lamb, bread crumbs, egg, onion, garlic, rosemary and salt and pepper, with a little cold water. Knead until everything is evenly incorporated.
Divide mixture and form into two 14x2-inches long roll.
Working with one at a time, place a lamb roll in the center of a pastry sheet. Brush all pastry edges with the egg mixture. Fold wide edges over the meat and press together. Make sure the seam side is on the bottom. Fold each end under the same way. Put roll on one side of the baking sheet.
Continue with the second roll and then put it at least 3-inches apart from the other one on the baking sheet.
Brush the tops with the egg mixture and make several diagonal cuts in the tops to let steam escape during baking.
Bake for 30 minutes or until the pastries are golden brown. Remove from oven and let the pastries cool.
Slice each pastry into ¾-inch slices and arrange on a serving platter.
These are tasty as is. Yogurt sauce (page 113) may be drizzled over the slices.
Pastries can be served hot or warm.

40 servings

Pot Stickers

I had the tastiest pot stickers on my first visit to San Francisco. They were savory and light.

After returning home, I signed up for the next Chinese cooking class, offered through the Vermont Culinary Institute in Montpelier, so that I could make them at home.

1 pound wonton or egg roll wrappers
2 cups Napa cabbage, finely shredded
1⅛ teaspoons salt, divided
½ pound ground pork
¼ cup scallions, diced
1 teaspoon grated ginger
1 teaspoon sesame oil
1 tablespoon dry white wine
½ teaspoon cornstarch
Pinch of pepper
2 tablespoons vegetable oil for cooking, possibly more

Cut the wrappers into 3-inch rounds.
Mix the shredded cabbage with 1 teaspoon salt, cover and set aside. After 5 minutes, or so, squeeze out any accumulated moisture.
In a bowl mix the cabbage, pork, scallions, ginger, wine, cornstarch, ⅛ teaspoon salt, sesame oil and pepper.
Assembly:
One at a time, put 1 tablespoon pork mixture in the center of a dough circle. Lift the edges above the mixture and pinch them together, forming 5 pleats as you go.
Heat a large frying pan – or a Wok - and when hot, lower to medium. Add 2 tablespoons of oil and fry each side until golden brown. Repeat until all dumplings are done.
Serve with dipping sauce.

24 servings

Dipping Sauce

¼ cup soy sauce
⅛ teaspoon garlic, minced
1 teaspoon sesame oil
¼ teaspoon vinegar

Blend all ingredients well.

Raw Snack Recipes
For friends and family with alternative diets.

Sunny Spread

½ cup walnuts halves
2 cups sunflower or pumpkin seeds, soaked in water overnight
1 cup chopped celery stalks
1 teaspoon sea salt
1 tablespoon olive oil
½ cup lemon juice
1 tablespoon dried basil, double if fresh
1 or 2 garlic cloves
Add 1 to 3 tablespoons water for desired texture

Blend all ingredients in a blender until smooth. Add the water in small amounts until the texture is to your liking.
Taste and add salt if needed.
Use it like any pate or dip.
This will keep in the refrigerator for up to a week.

Raw Cacao Bliss Balls

2 cups raw cacao powder
½ cup raw almond butter
½ cup chopped raisins
1 teaspoon vanilla
½ teaspoon stevia

In a bowl blend all ingredients until mixed well and sticking together. Roll into small balls and refrigerate until serving.

Raw Apricot Bliss Balls

2 cups dried apricots
½ cup tahini
1 tablespoon ginger powder
Dried coconut flakes

Mix first three ingredients in a blender until smooth. Add a little water if too stiff. Shape batter into desired size balls and roll in coconut flakes.
Refrigerate until needed.
The balls can be frozen and thawed a few at a time.

Steak Tartar

Meat was scarce at home in Berlin where I grew up.
When my mother planned to make steak tartar, she would announce at breakfast, "I'm making tartar tonight." I was then looking forward to one of my favorite dinners all day.
Three of us shared a quarter pound and made it last as long as we possibly could.
It is now one of my families' favorite also.

½ pound chopped beef, mince a steak yourself or buy the best freshly ground sirloin
½ small onion, minced
1 egg
2 tablespoons capers, minced
Salt and freshly ground pepper to taste
1 teaspoon brandy
Serving with:
1 dill pickle, cut into thin slices
Toasted French bread slices
German pumpernickel bread slices cut into quarters
Unsalted butter

Just before serving mix the first six ingredients.
Divide, form into four 1-inch high rounds and transfer to individual plates. Cover tops with dill pickle slices. Surround with buttered light and dark bread slices.

This serves 4 as appetizer, double amounts if is to be the main dish.

Steamed Mussels

From the ocean directly into a pot is the absolute best way to enjoy mussels.
If you are lucky to spend time at a rocky beach, you can harvest mussels at low-low tide. Mussels attach themselves to the bottoms of rocks near the ocean floor and it takes low tide to find them.
Ordering steamed mussels at a sea side restaurant or buying them fresh from a seafood purveyor are the next best alternatives.

Basic method:
Buy ½ pound mussels per person
1 garlic clove, diced
1 lemon, juiced
Water

Scrub the mussels in lots of water.
Put ½-inch of water, lemon juice and garlic in a large pot. Add the mussels and bring to a boil. Simmer until all mussels are open.
Divide mussels into individual bowls.
Serve a dipping sauce in small bowls alongside.

The most traditional sauce is melted butter and lemon juice.
For a lighter sauce make lemony vinaigrette.

Stuffed Mushrooms

Originally, I made the stuffing for this popular appetizer from scratch. Since then I've found that using quality ready-made sausage brings equally satisfying results.

2 tablespoons vegetable oil
18 white mushroom caps, medium size
1 pound sweet Italian sausage
Provolone slivers (optional)

Preheat oven to 375°F. Line a rimmed baking sheet with parchment paper.
Peel mushroom caps. Dip the top of cap quickly in oil. Put top of cap down on the baking sheet. Squeeze enough sausage out of casings to fill caps with a slight mound. (Freeze leftover sausage for future use.)
If desired, press a couple of provolone slivers onto filling.*
Bake in middle of oven for 15 minutes or until filling starts to brown.

6 Servings (3 per person for a buffet of mixed appetizers)

(*Can be made ahead to this point.)

Soups and Sauces

Basic Broth	20
Winter Broth	20
Egg Drop Soup	20
Black Bean Soup	21
Black Forest Chowder	22
Country Style Tomato Soup	23
French Onion Soup	24
Lentil Soup	25
Mayonnaise	25
Sopa de Ajo	26
Spicy Carrot Soup	27
Gravy Demystified	28
White Sauce	28
Brown Sauce	29
Turkey Gravy	29
Bacon Sauce	30
Pesto Sauce	30
Mock Hollandaise	31
Quick Tomato Sauce	32
Raw Tomato Sauce	32
Spaghetti Sauce	33

Soups or stews kept us going, summer and winter, when I was growing up in Berlin. I never tired of them. I love them still, whether as the starter or the main course.

Although this is not a how-to cookbook, I'm including instructions for sauce and gravy making. Sauces are the building blocks of a variety of dishes. Some of my friends were fearful of making gravies and I suspect many cooks still are. When I became a cook – before I gained experience – my earliest lessons were all about sauces.

Basic Broth
This is the same procedure for all basic broths.

2 beef bones or assorted chicken giblets
6 cups water
1 large onion, peeled
6 cloves, pressed into onion
1 large carrot, peeled and quartered
1 large celery stalk, quartered
1 bay leaf
Salt and pepper

In a saucepan large enough to hold all, cover bones/giblets with water.
Add remaining ingredients and bring to a boil.
Add salt and pepper to your preference, cover and simmer for at least 1 hour – longer will improve flavor.
Remove the vegetables and store the broth in the refrigerator or freeze in small amounts for future use.

Winter Broth
The best cold chaser I know.

4 cups beef broth* – see basic broth above
½ cup pasta – any small variety**
Freshly ground pepper
½ cup fresh Italian parsley, finely chopped

Bring broth to a boil. Add pasta and simmer until done. Adjust taste. Ladle into bowls. Top each serving generously with pepper and one tablespoon parsley.
When marrow bones are included, remove them before serving to extract the marrow. Slice marrow thinly and serve on toast sprinkled lightly with salt and pepper.
Servings depend on portion size.
(* When buying beef bones look for some that include shin bones with marrow.)

**For *Egg Drop Soup* omit pasta: In a bowl blend 2 tablespoons water with 2 eggs, stir vigorously into hot broth until eggs are solidified into shreds. It just takes 1 minute or so.
4 servings

Black Bean Soup

I first had this delicious soup on a sunny seaside deck in St. Thomas, Virgin Islands. We were on a winter reprieve, waiting for a ferry to take us to St. John. It became a staple in my soup repertoire.

2 tablespoons vegetable oil
1½ cups onions, diced
8 garlic gloves, minced
½ cup jalapenos, diced, seeds removed
2 cups dried black beans
1 tablespoon cumin
1 tablespoon coriander
8 cups vegetable stock or water
Salt and pepper to taste
1 cup fresh cilantro, chopped
Lime wedges for serving

Heat oil over medium in a large stew pot. Add onion and jalapeno and sauté for about 5 minutes.
Push mixture to sides, add garlic to center and stir until fragrant.
Add liquid, beans and spices and bring to a boil. Cover, reduce heat and gently simmer for 2 to 3 hours or until beans are tender. Time depends on the beans.
Add salt and pepper to taste, then add cilantro before serving.
If the soup gets refrigerated add additional cilantro after reheating.

8 servings

Black Forest Potato Chowder

I entered this recipe in a contest sponsored by *Better Homes and Gardens* magazine in 1970. It garnered an honorable mention. The prize was their 18-volume *Encyclopedia of Cooking*, a valued addition to my cookbook library.

The chowder makes a hearty lunch or dinner with pumpernickel bread and a salad.

Soup:
8 cups beef broth – see basic broth page 20
1 pound red potatoes, peeled and cut into ¼-inch cubes
2 carrots, peeled and diced – as above
3 tomatoes, diced
3 leeks, white and green parts sliced thin crosswise
½ celery root, diced – celery can be substituted
3 sprigs fresh parsley
1 small bay leaf
Salt and pepper to taste
4 tablespoons sour cream

Croutons:
4 thick slices pumpernickel or rye bread
1 slice thick bacon

Add all soup ingredients, except sour cream, to boiling broth. Bring to boil again while stirring occasionally. Reduce heat, cover and simmer for 30 minutes or until veggies are done.

Meanwhile prepare croutons. Dice bacon and fry. Cut bread into ½-inch cubes, add to the frying pan. Toss until bread is crisp. Set aside.

When vegetables are tender, but not falling apart, remove bay leaf and parsley.

In a small dish add a little broth to the sour cream, blend until smooth and add to soup. Simmer until heated through again, adjust taste if needed.

Ladle into bowls and top each serving with croutons and bacon.

4 to 8 servings

Country-Style Tomato Soup

A hearty, chunky soup that provides a satisfying lunch when served with pumpernickel bread and a crunchy salad.

2 tablespoons vegetable oil
2 medium onions, chopped
2 medium carrots, diced
2 tablespoons all-purpose flour
2 pounds Roma tomatoes, peeled and quartered
4 cups water
Salt and pepper to taste
½ cup fresh parsley, chopped
1 cup angel hair pasta, broken into 1-inch pieces
1 tablespoon fresh parsley, minced, for serving

Sauté onions and carrots in oil over medium heat until softened.
Add flour and stir to make a roux. Add tomatoes and mix well. Add water and bring to a boil while stirring to loosen any mixture from bottom of pan. Blend in salt, pepper and parsley. Cover and simmer for 45 minutes.
Add pasta, bring to boil again and simmer for another 10 minutes or until pasta is done.
Ladle into bowls and sprinkle with minced parsley.

6 to 8 servings

French Onion Soup

This French classic is never out of favor. It is simple to make. With basic components at hand it is quickly assembled and ready to go into the oven for the final step.

3 large onions, chopped
2 tablespoons unsalted butter
Salt and pepper to taste
4 cups beef or veggie broth
1 egg yolk mixed with 1 tablespoon red wine
4 slices French bread, toasted
1 tablespoon garlic butter – page 9
4 tablespoons grated Swiss or parmesan cheese

Sauté the onions in butter in a heavy bottomed soup pot over low heat. Onions should get very soft but not take on any color. It will take about 30 minutes.
Add the broth, bring to a boil, reduce heat, cover and simmer for 20 minutes. Add salt and pepper and taste.*
Meanwhile toast the bread and turn on the oven grill.
Remove soup pot from heat. Mix egg yolk and wine in a cup and stir into the soup.
Ladle the soup into individual oven proof serving bowls. Spread garlic butter onto toast and sprinkle with a tablespoon of grated cheese. Top the soup with toast, cut to fit if needed.
Put soup bowls on a rimmed baking sheet, slide it under the grill. Bake until the cheese is browned.

4 servings

(*The soup can be prepared well ahead of time to this point, even several days and refrigerated.
Bring the soup back to simmer before removing from the heat and continuing with the recipe.)

Lentil Soup
Most satisfying on a blustery day.

2 tablespoons vegetable oil
1 large onion, chopped
1 medium carrot, peeled and diced
4 cups water or vegetable or chicken stock, possibly more
1 cup dried lentils
1 bay leaf
1 teaspoon dried marjoram
Salt to taste
2 tablespoons vinegar or lemon juice
Lemon zest, grated – to taste
Freshly ground pepper

In a soup pot sauté the onions in oil over moderate heat for 5 minutes. Add carrots and cook another 5 minutes.
Add water, lentils, bay leaf, marjoram and salt and bring to a boil. Turn heat to low, cover and simmer for 1 hour or until lentils are done, soft but not falling apart.
Add vinegar, mix and taste.
Add lemon zest and freshly ground pepper to taste.

4 to 6 servings

Mayonnaise
Simple to make and the only way to be sure of ingredients.

1 egg yolk
1 teaspoon mustard
¼ teaspoon salt
1 tablespoon lemon juice
¾ to 1 cup of good oil

Have all ingredients at room temperature. Mix the first four ingredients in a bowl with a whisk until smooth.
While whisking, add the oil one drop at a time. When the mixture is thickening the oil can be added in a light stream. You may not need all the oil; mayonnaise is done when the mixture reached the desired volume.
Mayonnaise keeps safely up to 5 days in the refrigerator.
1 cup

Sopa de Ajo

I recreated the recipe after tasting Sopa de Ajo in a small cafe on the Costa Brava, in northern Spain. I never had a 'mostly garlic' dish before. It was in 1961, Spain just began developing the coastline for tourism. Our group stayed in one of the first high rises. It wasn't quite finished and the rates were marvelously low and the food was interesting everywhere! This soup always takes me back there.

1 Baguette – sourdough; at least a day old (or oven dry at very low heat) cut into 1-inch cubes
½ cup olive oil
1 large onion, chopped
8 large garlic cloves chopped – use more if you like
8 cups stock (I use organic veggie cubes if I don't have broth on hand)
8 New Mexico dried peppers, seeded and broken into large pieces
Salt and pepper to taste

Heat oil to medium in a stock pot, add onion and sauté until softened, about 10 minutes.
Add garlic and sauté for 1minute, then add bread cubes and all crumbs and stir until bread gets crunchy, take care not to burn the garlic.
Add stock and all peppers, bring to a boil, turn down heat to low and simmer for 2 hours or more. Soup will thicken.
Try to take out all pepper pieces and put into a blender with some soup liquid, blend until skins are basically pulverized. Return all back into soup, stir well.
Taste and add salt and pepper if needed.
Soup's ready!

4 to 6 servings

Try making it ahead, the soup is even better reheated.

Spicy Carrot Soup

Carrots were always abundant in my garden. This was one way of using them fresh.

1 tablespoon unsalted butter
1 medium yellow onion, diced
2 garlic cloves, more if they are tiny
8 carrots, peeled and cut into chunks
1 russet potato, peeled and cut into chunks
2 tablespoons fresh ginger, julienned
1 tablespoon fresh thyme
½ tablespoon cumin
½ tablespoon curry
1 cup dry white wine
5 cups veggie broth
1 lemon, juiced
Salt and pepper

Melt butter in a large pot and sauté onion over medium for 5 minutes. Add carrots, potato, ginger, thyme, cumin and curry and sauté for about 15 minutes over low heat, stirring occasionally. Add garlic and stir for a minute.
Add wine, stir well and let mixture come to boil. Add broth and lemon juice and bring to a boil again. Reduce heat and simmer, covered, for 30 minutes.
Puree the soup* and add salt and pepper to taste.

6 to 8 Servings

(* An immersion blender is the perfect tool here.)

Gravies and Sauces Demystified

I've met several frustrated cooks lamenting their lumpy gravies and sauces.
I offer this primer for future successes.

Basics for making a sauce or gravy are the same:
1: Heat your fat source over medium heat in a pan that's not too small –you'll need room to whisk in, or too big – a wider surface is harder to control when adding the liquid.
2: Add flour and stir and blend. Be ready to add the liquid when the flour reached the desired color – depends on the sauce being made.
3: Lower the heat and add the liquid in a small stream while whisking. When at least half of the liquid has been added, return the heat to medium and whisk while the sauce begins to thicken.
Keep adding liquid, a bit at a time, until the sauce reach the desired consistency.
Lower the heat again and simmer for another 10 minutes.

Sauce is usually made with butter or oil – **Gravy** utilizes pan drippings. Samples follow.

Basic White Sauce

2 tablespoons unsalted butter
2 tablespoons flour
1 cup milk or cream, or a combination
Salt and pepper

Melt the butter in a small sauce pan and stir in the flour. Blend well over low heat and then slowly add the liquid while stirring. Bring the sauce to a boil and then simmer for a couple of minutes while gently stirring. Add salt and pepper to taste.
This basic sauce can be used many ways by adding different herbs, spices, wine, etc.
Quantities may be multiplied for larger batches of sauce.

Basic Brown Sauce

2 tablespoons unsalted butter
½ small onion, quartered
2 tablespoons all-purpose flour
⅛ teaspoon salt
⅛ teaspoon ground pepper
1 cup beef broth or water

Melt the butter, add the onion and cook over low heat until the butter is starting to turn light brown.
Add the flour, salt, pepper and blend. While stirring, gradually add the liquid and bring to a boil. Simmer for 5 minutes, and then remove the onion. Continue to simmer for another 15 minutes.
This basic brown sauce also can turn into a variety of uses by adding curry, wine, ketchup, etc.

Turkey Gravy

4 tablespoons pan drippings
3 tablespoons all-purpose flour
2 cups turkey broth (made from giblets while the turkey was roasting, see broth recipe page 20)

Scrape drippings from the roasting pan and reheat them in a sauce pan. Add the flour and stir to blend over medium heat. Stir for a few minutes taking care not to burn the flour.
Slowly add the broth while stirring. Stir until the sauce is coming to a boil. Reduce heat to very low and simmer for at least 15 minutes.
Add more broth if the gravy is too thick.
Taste before serving.

The method is the same regardless of the dripping's source.

Bacon Sauce

This sauce, spooned over rice, dumplings or gnocchi, makes a tasty light dinner accompanied by a mixed salad.

¼ pound pancetta, diced (buy pancetta in ¼-inch slices)
2 tablespoons vegetable oil
½ onion, minced
2 tablespoons all-purpose flour
½ cup dry white wine
½ cup bouillon
½ cup sour cream
2 tablespoons fresh Italian parsley, minced
Freshly ground pepper to taste

Heat the oil over medium heat in a skillet. Add pancetta and slowly brown, stirring occasionally.
Add flour and stir until it is starting to take on a little color.
Immediately add wine while stirring. As the mixture thickens add bouillon and sour cream.
When the sauce starts to bubble, lower the heat, cover and simmer for about 20 minutes.
Add more bouillon if the sauce gets too thick. It should have a texture like heavy cream.
Taste. Depending on spiciness of the pancetta, the sauce may need salt and pepper. Add parsley, mix well and serve.
4 servings

Pesto Sauce

Make batches of pesto as fresh basil is available. Large plastic containers of basil often come on the market and are a better buy than the small ones containing 2 or 3 little branches.

5 cups fresh basil leaves, minced
½ cup Italian parsley, minced
¾ cup olive oil, more if needed
4 tablespoons garlic, finely minced
½ cup pinion nuts (optional)
½ teaspoon salt
½ cup parmesan, freshly grated

Mix all ingredients well. Spoon what is not immediately used into a mason jar. Pack tightly and cover with ½ inch olive oil.
Store in the refrigerator, it'll keep for at least a month.

Mock Hollandaise

This is a lighter version, same lemony taste, than a traditional Hollandaise. I serve it often whenever Hollandaise is called for; asparagus, broccoli, cauliflower, steak and fish come to mind.

4 tablespoons unsalted butter
2 tablespoons all-purpose flour
1½ cups veggie broth, maybe more
3 tablespoons lemon juice
Salt and pepper to taste
3 egg yolk mixed with an additional tablespoon lemon juice

In a saucepan heat the butter over medium heat. Add the flour and mix well. Lower the heat and cook the mixture for 5 minutes while stirring. Take care not to let the flour take on any color.
Slowly add the broth, turn up the heat again and bring the sauce to a low boil and simmer another 5 minutes. Add salt, pepper, 3 tablespoons lemon juice and bring to a simmer again. If the sauce gets too thick add a little more broth, until the sauce has the consistency of heavy cream.
Mix the egg yolks with the remaining lemon juice in a cup.
Remove sauce pan from heat and add the egg yolks while stirring.
Put the sauce pan back on the stove and stir over very low heat. The sauce will thicken. Remove pot from heat before the sauce reaches the simmer stage.

Makes 2 cups

Quick Tomato Sauce

A fragrant and quickly prepared alternative to the traditional spaghetti sauce. See the next recipe for an even faster option.

3 tablespoons olive oil
3 cloves garlic, julienned
8 Roma tomatoes, diced
⅛ teaspoon salt
Freshly ground pepper
¼ cup fresh basil, chopped*

Heat oil over low and add garlic. Soften garlic while stirring, about 2 minutes.
Turn heat to medium and add tomatoes and salt. Bring to a simmer. Cover dish and cook until tomatoes soften but are not totally falling apart, approximately 5 minutes.
Add basil and pepper, mix and serve.
(* Optional, it is loaded with flavor without basil also.)

4 servings

Raw Tomato Sauce

It doesn't get faster than this. An ideal recipe to turn to on hot summer evenings.

8 ripe tomatoes, chopped
¼ cup fresh basil, minced
¼ cup fresh parsley minced
2 tablespoons capers, diced
4 tablespoons olive oil
2 tablespoons balsamic vinegar
Freshly ground pepper
½ cup grated parmesan cheese for serving

Mix all ingredients, except parmesan, as much in advance as possible in a serving bowl.
Cook your favorite pasta al dente, drain and add to tomato sauce. Let sit for a minute and then toss really well and serve.
Pass a bowl with grated parmesan to sprinkle on top.

4 to 6 servings

Heidi's Spaghetti Sauce

Spaghetti sauce was one of the first Italian recipes I learned in the early 1960's. Cooking in Basel was the gateway to many culinary firsts. The menu leaned heavily on French and Italian cuisine. Today all Italian foods are favorites in my kitchen.

2 tablespoons vegetable oil
2 onions, chopped
1 green pepper, chopped
6 garlic cloves, minced
2 14-ounce cans peeled plum tomatoes, cut into quarters
A pinch of sugar
1 bay leaf
3 teaspoons dried basil
2 teaspoons dried thyme
2 teaspoons dried oregano
1 teaspoon dried tarragon
½ teaspoon ground fennel
1 cup dry red wine
1 6-ounce can tomato paste
Salt and pepper to taste
Grated Parmesan for serving

Heat the oil in a large saucepan and sauté onions and pepper over medium heat for 5 minutes. Add garlic, stir to mix and continue cooking for 2 minutes.
Add tomatoes, sugar, all herbs and wine. Bring to a simmer and cook for 30 minutes over low heat with lid askew.
Add tomato paste, salt and pepper and cook for another 30 minutes.*
Serve over favorite pastas, gnocchi or polenta.
Pass grated parmesan separately.

Makes 1 quart

(*Sometimes I add mild Italian sausages at this point and let them simmer along for 30 minutes. The amount depends on need.
I add 1 or 2 sausages per person if I serve them whole.
1 sausage per person if I slice and return them to the sauce.)

Breads & Crêpes

Crusty Italian Loaf	36
Focaccia	37
Irish Soda Bread	38
Oatmeal Bread	38
French Bread	39
Garlic Bread	40
European Rolls	40
Italian Rosemary Loaf	41
Rye Bread	42
Sandwiches	43
Italian Sub	44
Whole Wheat Bread	44
Crêpes	45
Stacked Crêpes	46
Savory Crêpes	46
Dessert Crêpes	46
Navajo Fry Bread	47
Navajo Taco	47

Why Add Water When Wine Will Do

In the years just after the war in Berlin, no one baked bread at home. None of our kitchens even had a baking oven. Instead, there were bakeries, sometimes two, on every block. The aroma of baking bread wafted out of the bakeries every morning. We happily bought fresh, crusty rye loaves daily.

When I moved to New York in 1963, packaged, spongy, white Wonder Bread was everywhere. Only a few ethnic neighborhoods offered more bread varieties. A couple of years later, in rural Vermont, options were limited. Occasionally a hefty rye loaf was imported from nearby Montreal. How I missed the fresh bread of my youth.

Then, in the 1960s I visited Werner Van Trapp's farmhouse in Waitsfield, Vermont. The aroma of baking bread was in the air. When I entered the kitchen, his wife Erika had just taken freshly baked loaves out of the oven. That was an "ah-ha, someday I'm going to try that" moment for me.

I found a bread-baking book with detailed instructions and started experimenting. Hefty whole wheat loaves, crusty rolls, light rye breads, French baguettes and many more varieties became standards in our house. I found that it was and is simple to incorporate bread making into daily life. Starting the process in the morning would result in fresh bread in the afternoon or evening.

Eventually I held bread baking sessions in my kitchen and passed my recipes and techniques on to others.

My husband Trent started baking bread also. His specialties are the hearty rye breads, made with well-aged sourdough starter. I happily leave those loaves to him.

Nothing says "home" more than a loaf or two of homemade bread baking in the oven.

Crusty Italian Loaf

When you absolutely do not want to spend time making bread, this is it. It so easy, you'll need an alarm clock not to forget about it. Do read the entire recipe, several steps are involved. It is a version of the newer no-knead method.
Adapted from a recipe featured in a Williams-Sonoma catalog.

3 cups all-purpose flour
¼ teaspoon active dry yeast
1¾ teaspoon salt
2 teaspoons fresh rosemary, minced
2 teaspoons lemon zest, minced
1⅝ cup warm water
Cornmeal as needed

In a large bowl combine flour, yeast, salt, rosemary and zest. Add the water; stir until blended (dough will be shaggy and sticky). Cover with plastic wrap. Let rest at room temperature, until surface is dotted with bubbles, 12 to 18 hours.
Sprinkle dough with flour in the bowl and punch down. With a dough scraper fold dough over onto itself a couple of times. Cover with plastic wrap and let rest 15 minutes.
Put a smooth cotton kitchen towel on a board and scatter cornmeal in the center where the dough will rest. Using very little flour, scoop the dough from the bowl and quickly shape it into a ball. Put dough, seam side down, on towel; dust with more cornmeal. Cover with another towel, let rise until dough is more than double in size and does not readily spring back when poked with a finger. About 2 hours.
At least 30 minutes before dough is ready, preheat oven to 450F and put a 2¾ qt. cast iron Dutch oven* in the oven.
Remove pot from oven when dough is ready. Slide a hand under the towel, turn dough over, seam side up, into pot.
<u>It's OK if it looks messy.</u>
Cover with the lid and bake 30 minutes. Uncover and bake until loaf is browned, 15 to 30 minutes more.
Slide the loaf out of the pan and cool on a wire rack.
1 loaf
(*If you do not have a cast iron Dutch oven – I have used a 12-inch cast iron pan and an upside-down springform pan as cover with great results.)

Focaccia

In Italy's Cinque-Terre region you'll see a Focacceria on every block. Bakers offer endless varieties of sweet or savory toppings. I like this one best.
Focaccia adapts well whether you use it for dipping in luscious olive oil or for making sandwiches.

1 envelope active dry yeast
1½ cups warm water
3 cups all-purpose flour
2 tablespoons olive oil
2 teaspoons salt
2 tablespoons fresh rosemary leaves, minced
Additional oil to cover dough
Topping:
1 tablespoon olive oil*
½ teaspoon coarse sea salt
(* Earlier, soak crushed garlic in the oil, remove before using.)
In a large bowl mix ½ cup warm water, ¾ cup flour and yeast. Scatter remaining flour over the top, do not mix. Set the bowl in a warm place until the moisture rises up through the flour.
Add the remaining water, oil, salt and rosemary. Using a dough scraper, mix right in the bowl, until the dough is smooth.
Hold dough in hand while adding enough oil to film bottom and sides of bowl. Return dough, turn over once so that it is lightly covered with oil. Cover bowl with plastic wrap. Let rise at least 8 hours, pinching it down once.
Punch down again and turn onto a floured board. Divide in half and shape into balls.
Put on a floured board, leave room for expansion, cover with saran and let rise again until doubled.
Put a baking stone on the bottom shelf. Preheat oven to 450°F.
Once dough has doubled, flatten each ball to 10" disk. Put one disk on a bakers peel (or rimless baking sheet) that's been dusted with cornmeal. Prick the disk all over with a fork and brush with olive oil. Sprinkle salt all over and very lightly press into dough.
Slide disk directly onto baking stone. Quickly throw 8 ice cubes on the bottom of oven and close the door.
Bake until Focaccia is lightly browned, 20 to 25 minutes. Remove to a cooling rack and repeat with second disk.

Irish Soda Bread

When I need a fresh loaf of bread fast, I turn to Irish soda bread or oatmeal bread - recipe below. Both are simple to make and delicious.

4 cups whole-wheat flour
2 cups all-purpose flour
¾ teaspoon salt
1 teaspoon baking soda
3 cups buttermilk

Preheat oven to 400F. Line an 8-inch cast iron Dutch oven with parchment paper, or a similar dish this size with a lid.
In a large bowl mix together the flours, salt and baking soda.
Stir in the buttermilk, making a dough that's not too wet or floppy. With wet hands shape it into a round loaf about 7-inches across and 2-inches high.
Set the dough in the skillet and cut a deep cross all the way to the edges of the top. Cover with the lid and place the dish in the middle of the oven.
Bake for 1 hour. Remove the lid and slide the dish back into the oven until the loaf is medium brown.
Remove from pan and let cool on a rack for several hours.
Makes 1 large loaf.
For a smaller loaf, cut all ingredients in half.

Oatmeal Bread

2 cups whole-wheat flour
1 cup oat bran
1 cup rolled oats (not instant)
1 tablespoon baking powder
¼ cup raisins (optional)
2 cups buttermilk

Preheat oven to 425F. Line a cookie sheet with parchment paper.
In a large bowl combine flours, oat bran, oats and baking powder, add raisins. Pour in buttermilk and mix with a large spatula. Flour your hands, shape the mixture into a 7-inch round loaf and place it on the cookie sheet. Smooth the top and make a deep X in the center. Dust the loaf with a bit of flour.
Bake for about 45 minutes or until the bottom sounds hollow when you thump it.

French Bread

Wonderful bread to accompany any meal. The loaves are ideal for making garlic bread or sandwiches.
The same method also makes European type crusty rolls that are sometimes hard to find.

1 envelope active dry yeast
1½ cups water, warm
1 teaspoon sugar
½ tablespoon salt
3 cups all-purpose flour
1 tablespoon vegetable oil
Corn meal for baking sheet
½ teaspoon salt
½ cup water
1½ teaspoons cornstarch

In a bowl combine the first four ingredients and stir to dissolve yeast; let stand for 5 minutes.
Stir in oil and flour and when dough is formed knead on a floured board until smooth and elastic. Cover with plastic wrap and let rise in a warm place until doubled in volume.
Punch dough down, divide in half and shape into balls. Let rest for 15 minutes. Shape each ball into a 15-inch oblong loaf, tapered at each end.
Sprinkle baking sheet generously with corn meal. Place loaves on baking sheet, far enough apart to allow rising without crowding. Cover with a towel and let rise for 60 minutes.
Preheat oven to 425°F.
Combine last 3 ingredients in a small pan. Bring to a boil and simmer while stirring until mixture is clear.
When ready to bake, brush mixture thinly onto loaves with a pastry brush.
Make 4 ¼-inch deep, diagonal slashes into each loaf – a razor works best.
 Slide the baking sheet onto the upper shelf, throw 8 ice cubes onto bottom and bake 10 minutes. Reduce heat to 325°F, throw an additional 8 ice cubes onto the bottom and bake for another 50 to 60 minutes. Loves should be a light golden brown.
Makes 2 loaves

Garlic Bread

Garlic butter at room temperature - page 10

Preheat oven to 375°F.
Cut any French or Italian loaf diagonally into 1½-inch thick slices, stopping ½-inch before the bottom.
Gently pry each slice apart and cover one side with garlic butter.
Press slices together again. Wrap the loaf with aluminum foil, but leaving the top uncovered. Put on a baking sheet and heat for about 10 minutes.

Slices get pulled off as needed.

Crusty European Rolls

These rolls will disappear quickly and you'll be making them again and again.

Follow the French bread recipe.

After the first rise, instead of making dough into oblong loaves, shape it into 3-inch long and 1-inch high rolls.
After final rise make a 2-inch slash into the top of each roll. Bake at 425° for 5 minutes and 375° for an additional 7 to 10 minutes or until rolls are golden brown.

Makes 10 to 12 rolls

The recipe easily doubles for either bread or rolls.

I save leftover rolls or bread. After a couple of days, when they are somewhat dried, I turn them into bread crumbs with a rolling pin.

Italian Rosemary Bread

A favorite for dipping or toast. Any leftovers make wonderful croutons.

3¾ teaspoons active dry yeast
1 cup warm water
1 cup buttermilk
⅓ cup olive oil
¼ cup fresh rosemary, finely minced
1 tablespoon salt
6¾ cups all-purpose flour
Cornmeal
Coarse sea salt

In a bowl stir yeast into water and let stand until foamy.
Add buttermilk, oil, rosemary and salt and blend.
Add flour gradually. When the mixture gets stiff, transfer to a floured board. Knead until all flour is incorporated and dough is smooth and elastic.
Transfer dough into a deep, oiled bowl and cover with plastic wrap. Let rise in a warm place until doubled, approximately 1½ hours.
On a floured surface divide dough in half. Shape each into a ball and put on a baking sheet sprinkled with cornmeal. Cover dough with plastic wrap and let rise for 1 hour.
Preheat oven to 425°F.
With a sharp knife or razor blade make an asterisk on top of loaves and sprinkle lightly with coarse salt.
Slide baking sheet onto a rack in the middle of the oven. Quickly throw 5 or 6 ice cubes into the oven to create moisture. Repeat again in 5 minutes. Bake the loaves for about 50 minutes or until bottoms sound hollow when tapped.
Cool completely before slicing.

Makes 2 loaves

Rye Bread
My non-sourdough version.

4 cups all-purpose flour
3 cups rye flour
1 tablespoon salt
2 envelopes active dry yeast
1 tablespoon vegetable oil
2½ cups warm water
Salt and water for brushing loaves

Mix both flours in a small bowl.

Combine 2½ cups of flour, salt, yeast, oil and the water in a large bowl. Stir vigorously with a wire whisk for a couple of minutes. (2 minutes at medium speed if using mixer). Add 1 more cup of flour mix well. Add additional flour to make soft dough. Knead on a floured board about until all flour is incorporated, 5 to 10 minutes.

Place in an oiled bowl and turn over once to get top covered with oil. Cover and let rise until doubled, about 45 to 60 minutes. Punch dough down and let rise again until doubled, approximately 30 to 45 minutes.

Punch down and turn onto board. Form two round balls. Place on a parchment paper covered baking sheet. Slightly flatten the top. Make a couple of slits with a sharp razor in the top. Cover with plastic wrap and let rise again until doubled, about 30 minutes.

Preheat oven to 425F

Mix 1 tablespoon salt and water each and brush both loaves.

Bake for 30 to 40 minutes or until golden brown.

Makes 2 loaves

The recipe is easily cut in half to yield 1 loaf.

Sandwiches

Picnic Sandwiches

Favorite Breads: Focaccia, French bread, Pita pockets
Bases: olive oil, flavored oils, mayo, mustard, salad dressing
Meats: Prosciutto, Mortadella, Salamis, Pastrami
Veggies: tomatoes, radishes, cucumbers, green or red peppers
Greens: arugula, romaine, watercress, sprouts
For the best tasting sandwiches, meats and veggies must be sliced paper thin. If they are falling apart, that's all right too. The more sides are exposed to oxygen the better the taste. Greens should be torn into small pieces.
Make sandwiches on whole loaves and then cut into serving sizes. All topping should extend beyond the edges.
Whatever your favorite combination, with these basics in mind, sandwiches will be delicious and also easy to eat.

My all time favorite to take on picnics is a prosciutto sandwich.
I drizzle garlic infused olive oil over both halves of a Focaccia loaf. I cover the bottom with thinly sliced and then shredded prosciutto. Top that generously with sliced tomatoes: grind fresh pepper over all tomatoes. Cover tomatoes with arugula or watercress.
Top all with the other half of the bread. Press down gently and wrap it tightly in foil or parchment until picnic time.

Open Face 'Afternoon Tea' Sandwiches

Bread: Pumpernickel, European rolls, rye
Base: Sweet butter, herb cheese, pesto, sour cream
Toppings: avocado, egg salad, cucumbers, radishes, tomatoes,
        pâtés, shrimp
Breads need to be covered all the way to the edges.
They should be cut into pieces that will take no more than two bites to finish.

Radish squares are my favorites. Cover a slice of rye with unsalted butter. Slice radishes paper thin and cover the bread with slices overlapping. Push slices slightly down, onto the butter so that they don't fall off when cutting into serving size pieces. Dust radishes with sea salt.

Italian Sub Sandwich

Always requested when everyone is at home.

4 sweet Italian sausages
2 medium onions, cut into eighth
2 green peppers, cut into ¼-inch strips
Vegetable oil as needed
4 small sub rolls

In a large pan sauté the sausages in oil over medium heat, turning them occasionally. After 10 minutes add the onions and peppers. Cook another 10 minutes, tossing the vegetables a couple times with a spatula.

Remove sausages. Leave veggies in the pan, turn off the heat. Slice the sausages into slivers at a strong angle.

Heat the rolls, cut them open, leaving one long side attached.

Divide sausages over the rolls and top with the vegetables.

Whole Wheat Bread

These loaves became a staple in my kitchen.

3 tablespoons active dry yeast
3 cups warm water
½ cup low fat milk, warm
2 teaspoons salt
2 tablespoons brown sugar
3 tablespoons vegetable oil
3 cups whole-wheat flour
3 cups all-purpose flour
¼ cup wheat germ
2 cups cracked wheat

In a large bowl dissolve the yeast in water; mix in milk, salt, sugar and oil.

Blend the flours, wheat germ and cracked wheat, then add to the liquid. Mix until smooth. Cover and let rise in a warm place until doubled.

Turn onto a floured board and knead a couple of minutes. Divide in half and shape into oval loaves and place on parchment paper. Let rise for 30 minutes.

Preheat oven to 350°F

Transfer parchment with loaves onto a baking sheet

Bake for 1 hour or until loaves are deep golden brown and sound hollow when tapped on the bottom.

Makes 2 loaves

Crêpes

Crêpes are tremendously versatile and easier to make – and keep – than you may think.

Batter:
1 cup all-purpose flour
⅛ teaspoon salt
4 eggs
3 tablespoons unsalted butter, melted
1 teaspoon lemon rind, minced
Approximately 1½ cups milk, more if batter gets too thick
Additional butter for crepe pan
An omelet pan if you have, a regular sauté pan with slanted sides, also works.

Make the batter about 1 hour before using it.
Mix dry ingredients in a bowl. Add the eggs, one at a time until the mixture is smooth. Add the melted butter and lemon rind. Slowly add the milk until the batter is the consistency of half-and-half.
Heat the oven to 'warm', put an ovenproof platter on the bottom shelf for storing crêpes.
Test the batter before heating pan. It probably needs a little thinning to that original mass.
Heat the pan a little hotter than medium. Grease with butter.
Scoop some batter with a cup. Tilt the pan about 10 degrees and start pouring the batter at the top, rotating while tilting the pan to assist the batter to cover the pan as thin as possible. Return excess batter to the bowl.
When the crêpe is getting brown around the edges, flip it with a spatula and continue browning the other side.
Put crepe on platter in the oven and cover with foil.
Repeat until all batter is gone.

Makes 18 to 20 crêpes

Stacked Crêpes Dinner

This works best with one kind of filling rather than a variety.
A fresh tomato and red onion salad on the side makes a colorful exclamation point!
Place a crêpe on a serving platter and spread your preferred filling over it – Creamed Spinach works really well.
Put another crêpe on top, pressing down lightly and continue until crêpes and sauce are done, but enough spinach mixture is left to cover the top.
A stack of 10 or 12 makes for good individual slices of the cake.
Cut into 8 slices.

4 to 6 servings

Crêpes can also be filled and rolled up. For individual servings, whether sweet or savory, everyone makes their own.

Savory Dinner Crêpes

A thick spaghetti sauce with browned ground beef works well. Mushroom sauce, sautéed vegetables or caramelized onions, are some of many other options.
Any creamed meat or vegetable sauce, meat cut into small pieces, would be perfect.
Offer as many different options as you are willing to prepare.
Serve these with a crunchy salad and there is a fun dinner.

Dessert Crêpes

Cherry or Raspberry sauces, or just whipped cream topped with chocolate shaving make tasty fillings. Spoon along one edge of the crêpe and roll it into a tube. Dust with powdered sugar.
Anything goes – be creative.

Navajo Fry Bread

This Southwestern staple is served many ways. I first tasted it as a base for Navajo Taco in a small diner in Tuba City, Arizona, on the way to Monument Valley.
I rarely make Navajo Tacos at home, but I serve fry bread often instead of corn bread.

2 cups all-purpose flour
2 teaspoons baking powder
½ teaspoon salt
1 cup warm water, more or less
Vegetable oil for frying

Mix flour, baking powder and salt in a deep bowl. Add warm water, little by little, and mix until you have soft dough.
Cover the bowl and set aside for 30 minutes.
Meanwhile cover a large frying pan with oil, it doesn't have to be deep, and heat it over medium high.
Divide dough into 12 equal pieces. One at a time, roll each piece into a 6-inch circle on a lightly floured board.
Cut a small hole out of the center of the dough and pierce the circle with a fork in several places.
Fry the circles on both sides until they are puffed and golden brown. They are best when hot.

12 servings

Navajo Taco

You'll need:
Crumbled and fried ground beef
Shredded lettuce
Diced tomatoes
Chopped onions
Red or green chile sauce.
Amounts depend on number of tacos to be made.

Each round of hot fry bread gets layered with beef, lettuce, tomatoes and onions. Top it off with chile sauce.

Pizza & Pasta

Basic Pizza	49
Thin Crust Pizza	50
Pizza Toppings	49
Fresh Pasta	52
Basil and Garlic Pasta	53
Manicotti	53
Mostaccioli	54
Pasta Carbonara	55
Presto Pasta	56

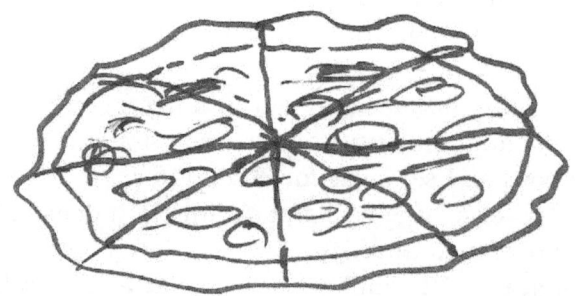

If our family did go out for dinner, it was to one of the Italian restaurants in Barre, Vermont.

Barre, known for its granite and marble quarries, has been home to a large number of Italians since the 1880s when stone masons from Italy first settled there. Barre was therefore a natural to support Italian restaurants serving excellent pastas and pizza.

I didn't make my own pasta until the 1980s, when one of the restaurant owners offered cooking classes. At first we met at his restaurant and then, years later, at the Vermont Culinary Institute in Montpelier.

What an eye-opener for me. We made mostly linguini and fettuccini. But sometimes we cut the dough into large rectangles instead, put a meat or ricotta filling on one end, rolled it up and called it manicotti. I loved manicotti. The filling and sauce combinations presented endless variety.

Make more pasta than needed, especially spaghetti or linguini. Leftover, refried pasta is divine.

Basic Pizza Dough

When ordering Pizza with "no cheese, please," in the early 70's, the request was met with stares of "WHAT?!" A very dry round, that was supposed to be pizza, then arrived at our table. So, we often made pizza at home.

It was the first meal that Jason made from scratch when the children took turns cooking one meal a week. He usually made extra to be sure there would be leftovers for his favorite breakfast.

1 cup warm water
1 envelope active dry yeast
3 cups all-purpose flour
2 tablespoons vegetable oil
½ teaspoon salt

Mix water yeast and 1½ cups flour. Add oil, salt and remaining flour (a bit at a time) in a mixer or by hand work the ingredients together until dough holds together. Knead on a lightly floured board until dough is elastic.
Transfer dough to an oiled bowl, turn over once to cover dough with oil. Cover with plastic wrap and let rise until doubled.
Punch dough down, divide in half and roll each into a ball. Set them on lightly floured board, not too close together, cover with wrap and let rest 15 to 20 minutes.
Cover pizza peel with parchment paper. Stretch and pull into 12-inch round. Place on peel and cover with toppings.
Baking temperature and times depends on the topping – see below.
Makes 2 crusts

Favorite Pizza Topping

1 12-inch pizza round
¼ cup tomato sauce or crushed tomatoes
3 fresh tomatoes, sliced thin
½ green pepper, sliced thin
½ cup onions, sliced thin
1 cup Italian sausage, browned and crumbled
½ cup crumbled Feta cheese*

Place pizza stone on lowest oven shelf. Preheat oven to 500F.
Spread sauce over dough, top with tomatoes and arrange toppings as desired.
Slide onto pizza stone and bake for about 15 to 20 minutes. Check frequently for doneness after 15 minutes.

* If using cheese, add it 10 minutes after putting pizza in oven.

Thin Crust Pizza

2 cups bread flour, plus extra for dusting
1 teaspoon instant (rapid rise) yeast
1 teaspoon salt
1 tablespoon vegetable oil, additional for brushing dough
1 cup warm water
Dough can be made in food processor. I usually make it by hand.

Mix flour, yeast and salt in a large bowl. Slowly add oil and water while stirring. When dough is starting to form a ball knead a few times right in the bowl.
Lift dough out of bowl, add a little oil and swish around.
Return dough and turn over once so that top of dough is oiled.
Cover with plastic wrap and let rise until doubled, usually 1 to 1 ½ hours.
After dough has risen, remove from bowl. Cut in half and shape each into a ball with floured hands. Place each ball on a lightly floured board. Cover with plastic wrap and let rest 10 minutes or so.
Cut two 20" length pieces of parchment.
Place pizza stone on lowest oven grate. Preheat oven to 475F.
With oiled hands stretch one dough ball into an 8x14 oval. At first stretch by holding dough at top and letting gravity help. Place on parchment, keep manipulating dough with your fingers until fully stretched and cover with favorite toppings.
Slip pizza peel under parchment and slide onto stone in oven.
Bake 10 to 15 minutes until deep golden brown.
Repeat with second pizza.

Makes 2 crusts

Favorite Thin Crust Pizza Topping

Topping for 1 pizza
Garlic flavored oil
1 cup caramelized onions or roasted Green Chiles, shredded
3 tomatoes, sliced thin
Freshly ground pepper
Grated parmesan

Brush dough completely with oil. Cover generously with onions or Chiles. Top with tomatoes, sprinkle pepper all over.
Ready to bake.
Remove when done and sprinkle with parmesan to your liking.

Always check on pizza before recommended done time.

Topping #2

2 tablespoons pesto sauce
3 tomatoes, sliced into thin rounds
2 mild Italian sausages, skins removed, sautéed and crumbled
2 ounces Mozzarella cheese, sliced paper thin and shredded
2 tablespoons fresh basil, shredded

Sauté the sausage in a frying pan in advance, breaking them into small pieces as they cook.
Spread pesto sauce within ½-inch of the edge. Cover with tomato slices. Top with sausage and mozzarella.
Bake on a pizza stone for 10 to minutes until cheese starts to bubble.
Remove pizza from oven, scatter with basil and serve.

I always by a chunk of Mozzarella, shredding it just before using.

Fresh Pasta

The first time I had pasta tossed with garlic, basil and oil, was the evening before a half-marathon race in 1983. The restaurant's large dining room was crowded with runners chowing down their pre-race favorite pasta dinner.

The race was competitive with stellar runners from the Boston area setting the pace. I had a personal best and gave most credit to this wonderfully light pasta dish. I have loved it ever since and make it often.

Basic recipe for 1 pound:
4 cups all-purpose flour
3 eggs
2½ teaspoons vegetable oil
½ teaspoon salt

Put flour in a large bowl and add eggs, oil and salt. Mix until dough is forming a ball.
Knead the dough on a floured board until smooth and elastic.
Cover the dough with plastic wrap and let it rest for 30 minutes.
Divide the dough in half. Place one on a floured board and roll it out to ⅛-inch thickness. Sprinkle dough with a little semolina and fold into along roll.
For Fettuccini* cut dough into ¼-inch wide strips. Dust strips with semolina and cover them with a kitchen towel. Repeat the procedure with the second piece of dough. Let the strips rest for 1 hour before cooking.
Bring water, 1 tablespoon of oil and 1 tablespoon salt to a boil in a large stock pot. Cook pasta in two batches as not to crowd it while cooking. When the pasta rises to the top start testing for doneness. It usually takes between 3 and 5 minutes.
When pasta is al dente remove all with a slotted spoon to a colander.
Boil the second batch and when it is done add the pasta to the colander.
Reserve a ¼ cup of the cooking liquid.

(*For Manicotti, cut the pasta into 3x4 rectangles.)

Basil and Garlic Pasta

A garlic lover's bliss.

1 pound fettucini or spaghetti
3 tablespoon olive oil
2 tablespoons minced garlic
⅛ teaspoon salt
Freshly ground pepper
½ cup fresh basil, minced

Cook pasta.
Heat the oil over medium heat and add salt and garlic and stir for 1 minute. Remove from the heat and let the mixture sit for 15 minutes, or longer.
When the pasta is almost done, reheat the oil and garlic mixture.
Put the basil at the bottom of a serving bowl, add the garlic mixture, a generous amount of ground pepper and blend. Add the reserved cooking liquid and, after a quick toss, the drained pasta. Mix well and serve immediately.
Pass a bowl with grated parmesan.
4 servings
Rustic Italian bread for dipping in olive oil, freshly grated parmesan to top the pasta, and a salad round out this dinner. Use pesto sauce instead for an even faster dinner, page 30.

Manicotti/Cannelloni

1 pound pasta rectangles see Fresh Pasta, page 52
Filling of your choice
1 cup tomato sauce
¼ cup parmesan, freshly grated

Cook pasta rectangles al dente and drain.
Preheat oven to 400F, grease a baking dish, large enough to hold pasta in one layer.
Spread filling along the 3-inch edge of cooked pasta and roll up. Cover bottom of dish thinly with sauce. Arrange filled pasta, seam side down, in the dish and cover with sauce. Sprinkle parmesan evenly over the top.
Bake for 15 to 20 minutes or until top is pale brown.
4 servings

Mostaccioli

It is equally delicious whether hot, warm or cold.

1 pound mild Italian sausage*
5 tablespoons vegetable oil, total
2 large onions, cut into sixteenth
2 green peppers, julienned ¼-inch width
4 medium sized zucchini, cut into thin slices
6 Roma tomatoes, cut into eights
4 large cloves garlic, cut into thin slices
3 tablespoons fresh basil, chopped
3 tablespoons fresh Italian parsley, minced
1 pound mini penne
Small amount of salt
Freshly ground pepper to taste
Grated parmesan

In a large frying pan, brown sausages in 1 tablespoon of oil and sauté over low heat until done. Set aside and keep warm.

Meanwhile, in another large pan, heat 2 tablespoons of oil over medium heat sauté the onions until they soften lightly. Mix in the green peppers, sprinkle lightly with salt and continue sautéing. After 5 minutes, add the zucchini, mix lightly and continue.

Select a serving bowl large enough to hold the finished dish.

While the veggies are sautéing, cook the penne al dente. When done, take ½ cup of the cooking water and pour it into the bowl. Drain the penne and add to the serving dish. Keep warm.

When the veggies have softened add them to the penne.

In the same pan heat one tablespoon of oil and sauté the garlic over medium heat. When the garlic is soft and fragrant add the tomatoes and toss with the garlic. Sauté 10 minutes or until tomatoes are barely done. Add the mixture, remaining oil, basil, parsley and 15 turns of ground pepper to the penne and mix thoroughly.

Slice sausages thinly, add to penne and blend into the mixture. Cover and let sit for at least 10 minutes. Before serving, mix the penne again and taste. Pass grated parmesan separately.

6 to 8 servings

*Equally tasty without sausage; increase garlic and basil to taste

Pasta Carbonara

Spaghetti is the more traditional pasta for this dish. Angel hair makes it lighter and also quicker to prepare.

This is as simple to make for one as it is for ten – ten just takes more muscle when tossing.

1 tablespoon olive oil
5 ounces pancetta cut into small dice
½ cup dry white wine
1 pound angel hair pasta
1 tablespoon salt
3 eggs plus 3 yolks mixed with ¼ cup warm water
½ cup freshly grated parmesan
Freshly ground pepper
1 tablespoon fresh Italian parsley, finely minced
2 tablespoons grated parmesan

Heat oil in pan over medium heat, add pancetta and fry until crisp. Add the wine and cook, scraping the bottom of the pan, for 3 to 4 minutes. Set aside.
In a small bowl mix eggs and water vigorously until smooth, set aside.
Cook pasta in a large pot until done. Drain in a colander and return to pot.
Add egg mixture, quickly toss.
Scrape pancetta mixture from pan into the pot and quickly toss with two spoons.
Add ½ cup parmesan and keep tossing until eggs barely start setting.
Add parsley and keep mixing until all liquid is absorbed. Add freshly ground pepper, toss again.
Sprinkle additional parmesan over each serving.

4 servings

Original Carbonara was not made with cream as it is often made today.

Presto Pasta
Heidi's Mac and Cheese version

A wonderful easy dinner for two accompanied by crusty bread, a crunchy salad and your favorite red wine.

1 cup mini penne
4 tablespoons unsalted butter
½ cup breadcrumbs
Coarsely ground pepper
1 cup grated parmesan
1 cup fresh Italian parsley, minced

Cook penne in salted water according to package directions.
At the same, time slowly brown the butter in a sauté pan.
Add the breadcrumbs when butter turns light brown and stir. Remove from heat when the breadcrumbs are medium brown. Cover and keep warm.
When the pasta is done, drain and divide evenly on two plates or wide dinner bowls.
Divide the parmesan evenly and sprinkle over the pasta.
Quickly grind pepper generously over both portions.
Reheat the breadcrumbs and spoon over the cheese.
Top with more freshly ground pepper.
Cover both portions with ample parsley.
The cheese will melt and blend with the pasta while everything is gently mixed on the plate before eating.

2 servings

I used to cook regular penne for this recipe. Since mini-penne has been introduced it is my choice for all penne recipes. I prefer the smaller size of the cooked pasta.

Salads

Belgian Endive Salad	58
Celery Root Salad	58
Cucumber Salad	59
Salad Dressing	60
Vinaigrette	60
Spring Greens with Goat Cheese	61
Sauerkraut Salad	61
Tomato Platter	62
Tomato Salad	62

To me, a meal without salad is unthinkable. The lettuce varieties offered today were not on the market twenty to thirty years ago. Now, thankfully, combinations for a simple salad are endless. Plus, salads can be satisfying enough to be the main course.

Lettuces occupied a good part in our extensive vegetable garden in Vermont. Planted in succession throughout the summer, ample portions were always available for picking.

At our much smaller home now in Taos, New Mexico, Trent and I grow a variety of lettuces. I raise smaller kinds, such as arugula, in containers. Mixed greens with chunky fresh tomatoes and slivered red onions, remains a favorite salad.

Many flowers are edible and can add variety and taste interest to salads.

A list of edible flowers is on page 186.

Belgian Endive Salad

This salad can be assembled several hours ahead, covered and refrigerated. Toss with the salad dressing just before serving. This is a welcome change from lettuce greens and a tasty stand-by.

4 Belgian endives*, remove hard, white bottom and cut crosswise into ½-inch slices
2 cups arugula, coarsely chopped
½ cup salad dressing (page 60)
Salt and freshly ground pepper to taste

Mix endives and arugula in a salad bowl. Toss with vinaigrette a few minutes before serving.
Add salt and a generous amount of pepper, toss again and taste for seasoning.

4 servings
(*Choose yellow endives with as little green as possible.)

Variation:
½ pound sliced button mushrooms instead of arugula and
½ cup fresh Italian parsley, minced

Celery Root Salad

Celery root salad adds variety to the appetizer repertoire or any buffet style luncheon or dinner.

4 tablespoons mayonnaise
2 tablespoon apple cider vinegar or lemon juice
Salt and freshly ground pepper to taste
3 cups celery root, finely grated – from 1 fresh celery root
½ cup fresh parsley, minced
½ cup finely chopped walnuts (optional)

Blend mayonnaise, vinegar and salt and pepper until smooth in a mixing bowl. Add grated celery root and mix.
Cover and let stand for at least 1 hour, can be longer.
Just before serving mix in parsley and walnuts and taste.
Add more mayo and vinegar if needed. The salad should not be dry but also not runny.

4 to 6 servings

German Cucumber Salad

The secret to a crunchy cucumber salad is to prepare it ahead of time.

2 medium to large cucumbers, peeled and sliced very thin
½ teaspoon salt
¼ cup sour cream*
2 tablespoons lemon juice
1 small onion, quartered and sliced very thin, or 1 bunch scallions cut very thin diagonally
Freshly ground pepper
2 tablespoons fresh dill, minced

Mix cucumbers and salt in a non-corrosive bowl, cover and let sit for at least 1 hour.
Drain off any accumulated juices.
Mix sour cream and lemon juice and add to the bowl, along with the sliced onions and ground pepper. Blend all and let sit for about 30 minutes, longer if possible for
Add dill, blend in and serve.

(* Yogurt can be substituted.)

4 to 6 servings

Salad Dressing

This is my dressing of choice when simply sprinkling olive oil and balsamic over my greens will not do.

1 cup preferred oil
⅓ cup cider vinegar*
1 tablespoon mayonnaise
½ teaspoon mild mustard
Salt and freshly ground pepper to taste
4 cloves garlic, sliced thin
1 pinch curry, more if desired

In large measuring cup blend oil and your favorite vinegar until smooth. Add mayo and mustard and mix until dissolved, add salt and pepper and taste. Add garlic slices and curry.
Really, a pinch of curry will do. You do not want it to scream CURRY! Cover and let sit for at least 1 hour before tasting again. Adjust flavors.
Pour into a jar and keep refrigerated until needed.
Remove garlic after 24 hours.

(* Experiment with substituting white wine for vinegar. It gives a more subtle taste.)

Yields 1 cup

Basic Vinaigrette

1 cup oil
⅓ cup vinegar or lemon juice
Salt and freshly ground pepper to taste

Mix these basic components well.
Add other herbs and spices to your preference.
I always have a jar of vinaigrette on hand that I spruce up depending on the salad I'm serving.

The recipe is easily multiplied.

Spring Greens with Warm Goat Cheese

Sprinkled with edible flowers like pansies or nasturtiums, this salad truly says spring.

8 goat cheese rounds, ¼-inch thick
¼ cup sesame seeds
8 baguette slices, toasted
4 cups mixed greens
8 tablespoons salad dressing

Preheat oven to 350ºF. Line a small baking sheet with parchment paper.
Coat goat cheese slices with sesame seeds. Transfer to baking sheet.
Bake for about 5 minutes or until cheese starts to bubble slightly.
Meanwhile divide greens into 4 equal portions on salad plates. Drizzle each serving with 2 tablespoons of salad dressing.
With a spatula carefully transfer warm cheese slices and place 2 on top of each salad.
Serve with baguette slices on the side.

4 servings

Sauerkraut Salad

A healthy stand-by in European kitchens.

1 pound sauerkraut, rinsed twice and drained
Salad dressing:
4 tablespoons vegetable oil
2 tablespoons white wine

Chop sauerkraut and mix with the dressing. Cover and set aside for several hours if possible.
Taste and add freshly ground pepper to preference. If the salad seems dry add additional white wine.

The salad can be made several days in advance and refrigerated.

Tomato and Mozzarella Platter

Fresh, ripe tomatoes are a must. I only make this salad when my tomatoes are ready or I can buy other, fully ripe, organic ones.

Slicing tomatoes*
Mozzarella or feta cheese
Olive oil
Salt
Freshly ground pepper
Fresh basil for garnish

Cut tomatoes into even slices. Slice the cheese as thin as possible.
On a serving platter alternate tomato and cheese slices in rows or circles. Drizzle thinly with the best olive oil available. Dust with coarsely ground pepper.
Just before serving garnish with basil leaves.

(*Amounts depend on need. I plan on one tomato per person for a small menu. One tomato half per person will suffice at a large buffet.)

Tomato Salad

The simplest and best way to serve ripe tomatoes at breakfast, lunch or dinner.

4 large round tomatoes – ripe but firm, cut into even slices
1 tablespoon olive oil
⅛ teaspoon salt
Freshly ground pepper
2 tablespoons minced red onion
1 tablespoon fresh Italian parsley, minced

Arrange overlapping tomato slices in circles on a serving platter.
Drizzle oil evenly over the slices. Sprinkle the salt lightly over the tomatoes and grind pepper on top.
Distribute the onions evenly over all slices and top with parsley.
Let the slices sit for at least 30 minutes before serving.

4 servings

Vegetables and Sides

Baked Whole Tomatoes	65
Caramelized Onions	65
Creamed Onions	66
Creamed Spinach	67
Stuffed Tomatoes	67
Curried Veggie Stew	68
Fancy Brussels Sprouts	69
Fennel Gratin	69
Green Beans á la Provence	70
Grilled Veggie Dinner	71
Kohlrabi	72
About Potatoes	73
Mashed Potatoes	73
Garlic Mashed Potatoes	73
New Potatoes	74
Potato Dumplings	75
Potato Pancakes	76
Potato Salad	77
Farro	78
Millet	79
Quinoa	79
Polenta	80
Tabbouleh	81
Mustard Pickles	82
Ratatouille	83
Red Cabbage	84
Roasted Garlic	85
Roasted Veggies	86
Sautéed Kale	87
Sauerkraut	88
Savoy Cabbage	88
Spinach and Rice	89
Sweet Potatoes	89
Tomatoes Provencal	90
Wild Rice	91
Zucchini with Dill	92
Onion Marmalade	92

Vegetables are the ultimate for simple, satisfying meals. The fresher the vegetable, the less fuss. Just a little butter or olive oil, some chopped fresh parsley, a pinch of salt and freshly ground pepper will bring out their best flavors.

One of my favorite dinners is steamed cauliflower, sprinkled with lemon juice, topped with browned butter and bread crumbs. With sliced tomatoes and some dark bread on the side, dinner is complete. Asparagus spears are delicious prepared this way also.

Fresh, of course, is key. Having your own vegetable garden is the best way to guarantee quality. When we bought an old farmhouse in Vermont in 1968, we immediately established a suitable patch for the vegetable garden. Across the driveway, beyond a couple of junk cars, was a sagging barn. Trent tore it down, tilled the earth, and we started planting. Later we learned that the sagging building was the cow barn, so our vegetables grew in rich soil indeed.

We literally raised every vegetable from A to Z - asparagus to zucchini. But we also learned that you don't need a half-acre size garden to raise veggies. I've raised crops in pots for several years, starting when we lived in a small condominium in Wilmington, North Carolina.

Now, in New Mexico, I'm continuing that practice because some varieties actually grow better in pots than in the heavy, native clay soil. Green beans, eggplant, peppers, tomatoes and even potatoes do very well here in containers.

Baked Whole Tomatoes

These tomatoes are a good balance when everything is garlicky and spicy.

4 tomatoes, as fresh as possible
Salt and pepper, a dash each – sorry just can't measure these small amounts
1 tablespoon unsalted butter, cut into 4 equal parts

Preheat oven to 375°F.
Moisten a baking dish with water or oil.
Cut a deep 1-inch cross into tops of each tomato. Gently squeeze the side of tomato and add salt and pepper into the gap. Insert a butter sliver.
Transfer to prepared dish and bake 15 minutes or until tomatoes are soft to the touch.

4 servings

Caramelized Onions

My mother treated me to a small steak topped with caramelized onions when I graduated from high school. It was a surprise. I never had a whole steak before and enjoyed the sweet tasting onions with it.

Now I sauté lots of onions not only for topping steaks, but also burgers, polenta, even pizza.

When planning a menu, keep in mind that this is a slow process. The onions can also be prepared earlier in the day and then reheated.

4 large onions
4 tablespoons unsalted butter
⅛ teaspoon salt

Peel onions, cut in half and slice very thinly horizontally. Heat butter in a large sauté pan, add onions and salt and stir until well coated. Sauté over medium heat until onions soften and slowly caramelize but do not burn.
This may take 40 to 50 minutes.

4 servings

Creamed Onions

This onion dish, along with the Thanksgiving sweet potatoes, is a holiday dinner must.

1 pound small white onions, or 2 10-ounce jars
Salt and freshly ground pepper
1 cup heavy cream

If the onions are fresh, peel and cook them until just barely underdone, approximately 20 minutes. Drain.
Since Thanksgiving is such a busy time I almost always opt for the jarred ones. Drain onions well.
Preheat oven to 375^0F.
Oil or grease a baking dish, deep is preferable over wide, to hold onions in several layers.
Arrange onions in the baking dish. Cover with the cream. Dust with a little salt and top with several grinds of the peppermill.
Bake for about 30 minutes or until cream makes a deep brown topping.
Cover with foil to keep warm while the other sides are being readied.

Multiple servings

Creamed Spinach

There is no cream in this recipe, although cream could be substituted for the water. It is creamy as is.

2 tablespoons vegetable oil
1 small onion, chopped
1 clove garlic minced
2 tablespoons all-purpose flour
½ cup water, more if needed
1 pound fresh spinach, chopped coarsely
Grated fresh nutmeg – a couple strokes on the grater
Salt and pepper

Heat oil over medium, add onion and sauté until it softens, approximately 10 minutes. Add garlic and stir for a minute. Add flour and mix until it is starting to take on color. Add water and bring to a boil while stirring. Add spinach and bring back to a boil. Cover, lower heat and simmer for 10 minutes.
Add nutmeg, salt and pepper and more liquid if necessary. The mixture should be on the thick side.
Simmer for another minute and serve.

4 servings

Make the mixture thicker and it can be used to stuff tomatoes.

Stuffed Tomatoes

A simple vegetable dish to prepare in large amounts.

4 round tomatoes, the same size if possible
Creamed spinach, make the sauce very thick
Grated parmesan cheese

Preheat oven to 350°F. Crease the bottom of a baking dish to hold tomatoes in one layer.
Cut off the top of the tomatoes. Scrape out the interior with a spoon. Turn tomatoes upside down for 10 minutes to let any juices drain.
Fill tomatoes with spinach to the very top and place them in the baking dish.
Bake in the middle of the oven for 20 minutes. Sprinkle parmesan cheese on top and serve hot.

4 servings

Curried Veggie Stew

Always on the lookout for a new one-dish meal, this recipe was adapted from India. I usually double the recipe for another tasty dinner.

2 tablespoons vegetable oil
1 large onion, diced
1 tablespoon curry
1 tablespoon coriander
1 teaspoon turmeric
1 large clove garlic, crushed
1-inch piece ginger, peeled and minced
4 cups water or veggie bouillon
3 large or 6 small Russet potatoes, peeled and cut into 1-inch cubes (size is not crucial as they are falling apart when finished)
1 small head cauliflower or ½ large, cut into florets
⅛ teaspoon salt and pepper each, to taste
2 cups frozen petite peas (a 12-ounce packet)
2 tablespoons fresh cilantro, minced

Heat oil to medium in a stew pot. Add onions and sauté until translucent, about 5 minutes, then add curry, coriander and turmeric. Stir until very fragrant, about 3 to 4 minutes.
Push mixture to sides, add garlic and ginger and sauté for a minute or so, do not brown. Add salt and pepper. Add water, bring to a boil; then add potatoes, bring to boil again. Simmer for 20 minutes.
Add cauliflower, bring to boil and simmer another 30 minutes or until veggies are done. Adjust seasonings to taste.
The potatoes should start to fall apart and thicken the mixture.
Green peas are added when ready to serve. Just add them, bring to a simmer and all is done (you want the peas to retain their crunch).
Add cilantro, mix and serve.

4 servings

Fancy Brussels Sprouts

This is different from most versions of serving this vegetable.

1 pound Brussels sprouts, cooked
3 tablespoons unsalted butter
2 tablespoons coarse breadcrumbs
3 hardboiled eggs – yolks only
2 tablespoons fresh parsley, minced

Cook Brussels sprouts to your liking, drain and keep them warm in a bowl.
Peel eggs and crumble the yolks, mix with the parsley and set aside.
Heat butter over medium in a small frying pan. When butter begins to brown add the breadcrumbs, turn up the heat and brown mixture while stirring until the breadcrumbs are a rich, golden brown.
Spread the eggs mixture over the Brussels sprouts and pour breadcrumbs on top. Serve hot.

4 servings

Baked Fennel

It was love at first bite.

2 fennel bulbs
1 cup half and half
Salt and freshly ground pepper
2 tablespoons unsalted butter cut into slivers
Butter for greasing pan

Preheat the oven to 350^0F. Grease a deep rather than wide baking dish.
Cut stems off the bulb. Cut fennel into quarters and then into ¼-inch crosswise slices. Blanch fennel for 3 to 4 minutes. Drain and spread them into the baking dish. Pour half and half into the dish until fennel is almost covered. Sprinkle with salt and pepper and dot evenly with the butter.
Bake for about 20 minutes or until tops are golden.

4 servings

This methods works as well with leeks, cut into 1-ich rounds.

Green Beans á la Provence

This was my mother's favorite green beans dish. She learned the recipe while helping in a French farmhouse kitchen. As a young woman she belonged to one of Hitler's mandatory youth groups. In the 1930s, youth groups were sent to help with the harvest in France. This was Hitler's way of showing good will. My mother suffered severe migraine headaches whenever she was outside in warm weather. So, instead of working in the fields, she was assigned to the kitchen. She loved that part.

To me, the acidity of the tomatoes brings out the best in the green beans. It is now my favorite way with green beans also.

1 pound green beans, strings removed, cut into 3-inch pieces
4 sprigs fresh summer savory, or 1 teapoon dried
2 tablespoons vegetable oil
6 Roma tomatoes, coarsely chopped
Salt and freshly ground pepper
½ cup fresh Italian parsley chopped

Cook green beans and summer savory in lightly salted water until barely done. Drain. Remove the herb sprigs and set aside until needed.
In a large sauté pan heat oil over medium heat, add the tomatoes and salt and pepper. When mixture begins to bubble, cover, lower the heat and cook 5 minutes or until tomatoes are soft.
Add green beans to tomatoes and mix well. Add salt and pepper to taste, cover and heat through.
When ready to serve add parsley and stir gently until well distributed.

4 servings

Grilled Veggie Dinner

2 large Vidalia onions, cut into 1-inch slices
2 small eggplants, cut into 1-inch rounds
4 small zucchini, halved lengthwise
2 green peppers, cut into quarters lengthwise
2 red peppers cut into quarters lengthwise
5 Roma tomatoes cut in half
Oil for brushing vegetables
1 cup Vinaigrette, page 45

While grilling, also cook whatever you'll be serving with the vegetables. I prefer quinoa mixed with fresh herbs.

Brush vegetables with oil.
Grill the vegetables over medium heat in the order given.
Remove vegetable to a plate and keep warm while the others are grilling.
Tomatoes are always last. They only need a couple of minutes on each side.
Arrange the vegetable on a large platter. Serve quinoa in a bowl. Pass the vinaigrette for spooning over the vegetables.

4 servings

Kohlrabi

Kohlrabi is a popular vegetable in Germany. It was nowhere to be found when I came to New York in 1963. I've had a vegetable garden since 1965 and kohlrabi is a staple like carrots.

4 kohlrabi bulbs, use greens also
2 tablespoons vegetable oil
Salt and pepper
½ cup veggie broth
Chopped kohlrabi greens
A touch of grated nutmeg

Remove large leaf stalks and discard, keeping the young, smaller ones. Remove greens from stalks and blanch them in salted water. Drain and when they are cool enough to handle chop them coarsely. Set aside.

Peel the kohlrabi thinly. The root bottom may be hard, cut the bulb off at that point. Cut bulbs in half and then in ½-inch slices and then cubes.

Heat oil in a large saucepan and sauté while stirring for about 5 minutes. Add salt and pepper and sauté for another minute. Mix in the reserved greens.

Add the broth, cover, lower the heat and cook for about 20 minutes. Just before serving add a pinch of freshly grated nutmeg.

4 servings

A Word About Potatoes

Potatoes are a staple in Germany. They are rich in nutrients and low in calories. My father had a potato business and after World War II my uncles did the same. I helped often and learned all about the spud. Many varieties are known, each used for different purposes. In the US potato offerings were limited to Yukon Gold and Russets until very recently.

Many potatoes sold on the US market show green areas. Those parts were peeking above the soil while growing. Cut the green parts out completely.

The green contains the toxin solanine and has a bitter taste. We're not eating enough potatoes to die from the toxin, but cut it out anyway.

Mashed Potatoes

The Russet variety brings the lightest, fluffiest results.

6 large russet potatoes, peeled and quartered
½ teaspoon salt
3 tablespoons unsalted butter, cut into small pieces
Milk, as needed
Freshly grated nutmeg

Cover potatoes with water in a soup pot, cover and bring to a boil. Lower the heat and cook for about 20 minutes. When they are done, drain them well.
Mash the potatoes, add the butter and let it melt.
Slowly add the milk while stirring vigorously with a flat wire whisk. When the mixture is smooth and fluffy, add nutmeg to your taste.
Serve hot.

4 to 6 servings

Garlic Mashed Potatoes

Simply add 12 peeled garlic cloves to the potatoes while they are cooking.
Proceed with the recipe above.

New Potatoes

True, new potatoes are a must. In Germany new potatoes are as anticipated as the first asparagus.

Usually they are only available in early summer at Farmers' Markets. Anything else does not have the same flavor or tenderness.

This only needs a green salad to complete a special early summer lunch or dinner.

3 pounds new potatoes
1 pound farmer's cheese*
½ cup fresh chives, finely chopped
4 tablespoons unsalted butter
Salt and freshly ground pepper

Rinse potatoes well and steam them in their skins.
Meanwhile prep small bowls with cheese, chives and sea salt for passing around. Butter, in a serving dish and the pepper grinder should be at hand also.
Serving:
Put potatoes in a serving bowl. Everyone helps themselves to potatoes and the accompaniments. Each potato is handled individually, either cut in half or quarters; skin on or peeled, then consumed with the preferred topping.
Sometimes just a little dab of butter is all it takes to bring out the most flavor of a young potato.

4 servings

(*If Farmer's cheese is not available, use cottage cheese. Put cheese through a sieve to have a smoother consistency. Discard any liquid that may have drained from the cheese.)

German Potato Dumplings

This is the most basic recipe. You can be creative and put a crouton or bacon bits in the center of the dumpling when forming. That is an option especially of the dumpling is the main meal – laced with Bacon Sauce or simply with browned bread crumbs and a salad.

2 pounds russet potatoes, boiled and peeled
½ cup all-purpose flour
2 eggs
Salt and pepper to taste – nutmeg optional

Peel the potatoes when cool enough to handle. Place in a large bowl and mash them. Make an indent in the center, add eggs and mix lightly. Scatter flour and salt and pepper over the mixture and incorporate thoroughly with your hands. If the mixture seems very moist add flour and work it in until it seems fairly dry but sticks together well.
Bring lightly salted water to a boil in a large pot - dumplings should not be crowded.
Meanwhile form the mixture into approximately 2-inch dumplings. Add them to the boiling water. When the water comes to a boil again, reduce the heat to a simmer. Cook the dumplings for 6 to 10 minutes. They are done when floating on top and look slightly puffed.
If you're not quite ready to eat they may be put on a baking sheet lined with wax or parchment paper and held in a warm oven, but no longer than 30 minutes.

6 servings

Dumplings may be formed up to 30 minutes before boiling – any longer and they may get soggy.

Potato Pancakes

Potato pancakes can be a stand-alone meal, topped with applesauce or sour cream with chives and salad on the side.

Any topping will make these pancakes disappear fast.

Potato pancakes was my mother's idea of *fast food*. She usually made them Saturdays, when she was grocery shopping for the weekend at the farmer's market and had less time for preparing the noon meal.

4 large Russet potatoes, peeled and finely shredded*
1 medium onion, peeled and shredded
2 eggs
5 tablespoons all purpose-flour
½ teaspoon salt
12 turns with the pepper grinder
Vegetable oil for frying

Preheat oven to warm to hold finished pancakes on a paper towel lined platter as they are done.

Put the shredded potatoes in a colander for a few minutes to let potato water drain. Then put a large handful at a time in a kitchen towel and squeeze out as much of remaining potato moisture as you can.

Put in a large mixing bowl, add onion and egg and mix thoroughly. Then add flour, salt and pepper and blend.

Heat oil in a large, 12-inch frying pan to medium.

Scoop potato mixture with a ¼ cup measuring cup, put in skillet and flatten to approximately ¼-inch thick with a spatula. Add as many scoops as will fit into the pan.

Fry for about 2-3 minutes or until golden brown and then flip over to brown the other side.

Place on the platter in the oven and keep warm.

4 to 6 servings

(* I grate potatoes by hand, giving a finer shred than using a food processor. As a result I can use a measuring cup for transferring the mixture to the frying pan. A large serving spoon works better when potatoes are shredded with a food processor.)

Potato Salad

Every region in Germany makes a slightly different version of potato salad. In Berlin, it is made with the addition of marinated Herring. My version – sans Herring - follows.

    Potato salad is traditionally served with sausages on the side. Mustard and horseradish are offered as condiments for the sausages.

3 pounds red potatoes, all similar size
½ cup mayonnaise
6 tablespoons oil
6 tablespoons pickle juice (from the jar)
1 tablespoon mild mustard
1 large onion, quartered and thinly sliced crosswise
2 dill pickles, cut in half lengthwise and thinly sliced
Freshly ground pepper to taste
½ cup fresh Italian parsley, minced

Cook whole, skin on, potatoes 'til tender, approximately 40 minutes. Drain and let cool.
Meanwhile mix the next four ingredients until smooth in a bowl large enough for the finished salad. Add onions, pickles and pepper and blend.
When cool enough to handle, peel potatoes, cut in half, or quarters if they are large. Cut into about ¼-inch slices. Add to the bowl and mix gently until potatoes are coated with the dressing.
Add parsley and blend.
Cover and set aside in a cool place.
Check after a few hours. If the salad seems dry make more dressing and add.
Just before serving, taste* and dust with a little minced parsley.

6 to 8 servings

Best done in the morning so that flavors have time to mingle.

(* Pickles provide enough salt, but do taste before serving.)

Farro Salad

This ancient Etruscan grain is being discovered again. Years ago I bought a bag of Farro in Siena. Today you can find it in most grocery stores' specialty food section or on the Internet.

1 cup Farro
3 cups water
2 ½ tablespoons olive oil
2 ½ tablespoons balsamic or wine vinegar
⅛ teaspoon salt
1 cup lima beans
1 cup peas
2 cups arugula, coarsely chopped
4 plum tomatoes, seeded and finely chopped

Combine water and farro in a medium sauce pan and bring to a boil. Reduce heat and simmer, partially covered for about 20 minutes, until farro is tender. Drain.
In a salad bowl combine oil, vinegar and salt. Add farro and mix well. Set aside to cool.
Cook lima beans according to directions. Just before they are done, add peas and bring to a boil. Quickly drain in a colander and plunge veggies into a bowl of ice water.
Drain and add limas and peas to farro. Cover and chill.*
Just before serving, add arugula and tomatoes and toss. Taste and add more salt if needed.

4 to 6 servings

(* Can be done several hours ahead to this point, refrigerate if served the next day.)

Millet

Just like rice, it stands alone as a side dish and is adaptable to just about any combination. It can be added to stuffings and stews, made into a salad or, like Quinoa, turned into a breakfast cereal.

½ cup millet
1¼ cup broth or water
Salt and pepper to taste

Heat a saucepan, add the millet and roast to light golden.
Add the liquid, bring to a boil, cover and simmer for 20 minutes or until all liquid is absorbed.
Remove from heat. Fluff with a fork, cover again and let stand for 10 minutes before serving.

4 servings

Quinoa

Quinoa is a welcome change as a side dish for vegetables and meat alike.

1 cup quinoa
2 cups stock or water
2 tablespoons unsalted butter
Salt to taste

Rinse quinoa and drain.
Combine quinoa and stock in a saucepan and bring to a boil. Reduce heat to low, cover and simmer until liquid is absorbed and quinoa is translucent, about 12 to 20 minutes.
Add the butter and toss.

4 servings

Polenta with Caramelized Onions

It is one of my favorite simple dinners served with a crunchy green salad.

4 cups water
1 cup coarse cornmeal
1 teaspoon salt
1 bay leaf
1 tablespoon olive oil

Start by preparing the onions - page 65 - since they take longer than Polenta.

Put water in a large, heavy bottomed saucepan. Slowly pour in cornmeal while stirring with a whisk. Add salt and bay leaf and bring to a boil. Add oil, lower heat and let mixture barely simmer for about 30 minutes. Stir occasionally and loosen any cornmeal sticking at bottom. When done, remove bay leaf. Turn off heat, cover pot and let sit for at least 10 minutes. Polenta will easily pull away from sides for serving.

4 servings

A quick tomato sauce, or a sausage or beef ragout also make excellent toppings.

Tabbouleh

During a recent visit to Amman, Jordan, I noticed that parsley was sold in crates - not by the bunch, at a farmer's market. "What are they doing with so much parsley?" I was thinking.

At a cooking class in a Jordanian home I found the answer while we were making tabbouleh. The proportions of ingredients have evolved since I first tasted it at an indoor market in 1970 in Montreal, Canada. Parsley is the main ingredient.

2 tablespoons bulgur
2 cups fresh parsley, chopped
2 scallions, diced including usable green parts
20 leaves fresh mint, diced
2 tomatoes, diced
1 tablespoon olive oil
1 lemon, juiced
Salt to taste

Soak the bulgur in cold water in advance until done, about 4 hours.
Mix bulgur and remaining ingredients in a bowl. Let the mixture sit for about 15 minutes, longer if possible.
Taste and adjust seasonings if needed.
Tabbouleh can be prepared well ahead of time. Do taste again just before serving.

4 servings

Multiply as needed.

Mustard Pickles

Take advantage of an abundance of cucumbers with this easy method.

3 cups water
6 cups vinegar
3 onions, peeled cut in half and thinly sliced
9 tablespoons mild mustard
2 tablespoons sugar
3 bay leaves
1 tablespoon dried tarragon
3 tablespoons fresh dill, chopped
20 medium sized cucumbers

In a large stainless steel or enameled pot bring the first eight ingredients to a boil.

Meanwhile peel cucumbers, cut in half and scrape out seeds. Cut lengthwise into ¼-inch slices.

Add to the boiling water and bring to a rolling boil again. Simmer only long enough until they start to look glassy. Turn off heat. When cool enough to handle, fill a large crock or glass jar with the pickles and cover completely with its liquid. If the jar doesn't have a lid, it can be covered with parchment paper and secured with string or elastic.

They may, but don't have to be refrigerated.

Ratatouille

From the Mediterranean region of France, Ratatouille is superb whether served hot, at room temperature or cold.

3 tablespoons vegetable oil
1 large onion, diced
2 green peppers, chopped
3 medium zucchini, cut into ¼-inch thick slices
1 medium eggplant, cut into ½-inch cubes
6 tomatoes, quartered
Salt and pepper to taste
1 tablespoon dried tarragon, double if fresh
4 cloves garlic, minced
3 tablespoons fresh Italian parsley, chopped
1 teaspoon tomato paste (optional)

Heat oil to medium, sauté onion and peppers about 5 minutes. Add zucchini and sauté another 5 minutes, stirring occasionally to mix.
Add eggplant, mix and add tomatoes. Add tarragon, a little salt and pepper, mix and cover. Simmer until vegetables begin to soften, approximately 15 minutes.
Add garlic and parsley, add more salt and pepper if needed and simmer until barely done, about another 15 minutes.
Taste, add additional parsley and tomato paste if needed.

4 servings

I usually double the recipe to have leftovers.

Red Cabbage

This version evolved from German and French traditional recipes.

1 medium red cabbage – approximately 2 pounds, shredded
2 tablespoon vegetable oil (or duck or bacon fat)
1 medium McIntosh apple, peeled and chopped
½ cup dry red wine, more if needed
7 whole cloves
½ pound chestnuts (optional)
1 tablespoon tart jelly (currant if you can get it)
Salt and pepper to taste

Heat oil over moderate heat, add cabbage and toss until heated through. Add red wine, when boiling lower heat to simmer, add cloves, apple, jelly and a touch of salt. Cover and simmer for 30 minutes. Occasionally. check for sufficient moisture, add more red wine if needed.
If available, add the peeled and coarsely chopped chestnuts along with the apple.
Taste and adjust salt and pepper.
The flavor is best when reheated at least a couple of times.

Serves 4 to 6, leaving plenty for another meal.

Roasted Garlic

An appetizer for garlic aficionados.

I was introduced to roasted garlic in the late 1980's on our first trip to Taos, New Mexico. We walked around the Plaza and this wonderful, garlicky aroma lured us to a little Deli.

    Within a few minutes we were being served outside at a small table. We savored the taste and happily left for home with the recipe, didn't know it was so simple.

2 large garlic heads
Olive oil

Preheat oven to 350°F.
Remove most of the garlic's outer skin. Cut top ¼ off the pointy end, exposing garlic.
Pour enough oil into a small baking dish to cover the bottom. Put garlic, cut-side down into the dish. Cover lightly with foil, leaving a few gaps to let moisture escape. Bake for approximately 30 minutes. Garlic should be soft and light brown, but not burnt.
Put each garlic cut-side up on a plate with several toasted baguette slice on the side.
Garlic cloves readily pop out of the skin and easily spread on toast.

2 servings

Roasted Veggies

A simple do-ahead side dish or winter dinner that will permeate the kitchen with delectable aromas.

Preheat oven to 450°F
2 pounds red potatoes, cut into 2-inch chunks
1 pounds rutabagas, peeled and cut into 1-inch cubes
2 pounds onions, peeled, cut into 1-inch chunks
1 pound carrots, peeled, cut into 2-inch long pieces
1 pound sweet potatoes, peeled and cut into 1-inch cubes
1 pound parsnips, peeled and cut into 1-inch cubes
30 garlic cloves, unpeeled
5 tablespoons fresh rosemary, crumbled
Salt and freshly ground pepper
2 tablespoons vegetable oil

In a large bowl mix all ingredients until vegetables are well covered. Divide mixture evenly over two baking sheets.
Roast vegetables until they are fork tender, about 1 hour.
I usually remove garlic cloves before they get crisp, after about 30 minutes.

8 servings

Sautéed Kale

Kale was a standard vegetable at our Christmas Day dinners in Berlin.

My mother started cooking kale a week before. We did not have a refrigerator, so she kept the pot with kale on the sill outside the kitchen window. She reheated it several times. When the kale was finally served, it was just right.

2 pounds kale
¼ pound bacon, diced if thick slices can be bought, leave slices intact otherwise
1 large onion, chopped
½ cup veggie broth, possibly more
Salt and pepper

Strip kale off any thick stalks.
Blanch kale for 5 minutes in a large pot with a minimum of water. Remove kale to a bowl with a slotted spoon. Reserve the water.
When kale is cool enough to handle chop all of it coarsely.
Brown bacon in a stew pot, add the onion and sauté until it is translucent. Add kale, broth, salt and pepper and mix. When mixture is bubbling, turn heat to low, cover the pot and simmer for 30 minutes. Check from time to time to see if additional liquid is needed.
Cool off and refrigerate.
Reheat just before serving.

6 to 8 servings

Sauerkraut
My favorite way to prepare Sauerkraut.

1 tablespoon vegetable oil
1 large onion, chopped
2 pounds sauerkraut, rinsed twice and drained
8 juniper berries
½ cup dry white wine, possibly more

Sauté onion in coconut oil over medium heat until it looks glassy.
Add sauerkraut and mix. Add berries and wine and bring to a slow boil. Cover, reduce heat and simmer for ½ hour. Add more wine if needed.
Sauerkraut can be made anytime and refrigerated.
Reheating improves flavors greatly.

6 to 10 servings, depending on portion sizes

Savoy Cabbage
As a side dish, it adds variety. Savoy cabbage is milder than white cabbage. When sautéing a sweet flavor emerges. I always use Savoy instead of regular cabbage.

1 medium head Savoy cabbage, shredded
2 tablespoons vegetable oil
Salt and pepper
Water as needed
Freshly grated nutmeg

Heat the oil over medium heat in a small stew pot. Add the cabbage and gently toss to wilt all of it. Add a pinch of salt and a few turns of pepper from the pepper mill. Lower the heat, cover the pot and sauté for about 30 minutes. In the beginning check every few minutes in case water is needed to cover the bottom of the pot. Cabbage will release some moisture but sometimes not enough.
Just before serving add some grated nutmeg and mix it in well.

4 to 6 servings

Spinach and Rice

A tasty side dish any time of the year. Sprinkled with parmesan it can stand alone as a satisfying entree.

2 tablespoons vegetable oil
1 small onion, minced
1 cup Uncle Ben's rice
1¼ cup veggie broth
1 10-ounce package chopped spinach - thawed, or 1 pound fresh, chopped

Heat the oil over medium and sauté the onion until slightly softened.
Add the rice and stir until all kernels are coated.
Add the broth and bring it to a boil. Add the spinach, stir well and bring to a boil again. Cover the pan, turn heat to very low and simmer for 20 minutes.
By using veggie broth additional seasonings may not be needed. Make a taste test before serving.

4 to 6 servings

For this dish I use Uncle Ben's rice simply because it takes less time.

Sweet Potatoes
One of many traditional Thanksgiving vegetables.

4 sweet potatoes, peeled and quartered
2 tablespoons unsalted butter
½ cup orange juice – more if needed
2 tablespoons rum or brandy

Cover potatoes with salted water and boil until done, approximately 20 minutes, drain and mash.
Add butter and orange juice and blend.
Add rum, mix well and taste.
Serve hot.

Can be done ahead of time and quickly reheated.

Tomatoes Provencal

The tomatoes pair well with grilled meats.

4 round tomatoes
½ cup breadcrumbs
2 garlic cloves, minced
Salt and freshly ground pepper
2 tablespoons fresh Italian parsley, chopped
1 tablespoon olive oil

Preheat oven to 375F.
Cut tomatoes in half, scrape out seeds and set upside down for a few minutes to drain any juice.
Meanwhile combine the four dry ingredients, add olive oil and blend.
Turn tomatoes over. Place a tablespoon of herb mixture into cavity of each tomato. Distribute any remainder evenly. Depending on size of tomatoes, additional herb mixture may be needed.
Transfer tomatoes to a dish large enough to hold all in one layer.
Bake for 20 minutes or until herb mixture is lightly browned.
Tomatoes can sit lightly covered until serving time.

4 servings

Wild Rice

One of my favorite recipes to make ahead when cooking for a crowd and all stove burners will be busy close to dinner time.

1 cup wild rice
4 cups water
1 teaspoon salt
2 tablespoons unsalted butter
1 large onion, diced
1 teaspoon freshly ground pepper
1 cup fresh Italian parsley, minced
Additional parsley if needed

Combine rice and water in a large saucepan, bring to a boil. Add salt, lower temperature, cover and cook over very low heat for 1 hour. Remove from heat.
In a pan large enough to hold the rice, melt butter and sauté onions until softened, may take 10 to 15 minutes.
Drain any leftover moisture from the rice. Pour rice on top of onions and carefully toss. Add pepper and parsley and mix well. Cover and set aside.
Rice will keep warm for at least ½ hour.

4 to 6 servings

Rice can be prepared earlier and gently reheated. In that case it may need a bit more parsley to add fresh, green color.
The recipe is easy to cook in larger amounts.

Zucchini with Dill

Fresh dill is a must to bring out the desired flavor.

4 small zucchini, sliced thin
⅛ teaspoon salt
1 shallot or small onion, halved and sliced thin
1 tablespoon vegetable oil
2 tablespoons fresh dill, chopped
Several turns from the pepper grinder

Heat the oil over medium heat, add zucchinis and salt and gently toss for several minutes. When zucchini begins to soften mix in the shallot, lower the heat, cover and simmer for about 10 minutes. The vegetable should be soft but not mushy.
Add dill and pepper, toss and serve.
Zucchini generates its own liquid, but do check every couple of minutes to make sure the bottom of the pan is moist. Add a splash of water if needed.

4 servings

Onion Marmalade

Onion marmalade is an excellent grilled meat topping.

1½ pounds red onions, cut in half and sliced thin
½ cup sugar
½ cup unsalted butter
Salt and pepper to taste
⅔ cup dry red wine
⅓ cup apple cider vinegar, plus 1 tablespoon

Melt the butter in a stainless steel pan, add onion, sugar, salt and pepper. Mix, cover and cook 30 minutes over low heat.
Add wine and vinegar and bring to a boil. Cook uncovered over moderate heat for 30 minutes, stirring occasionally. Continue cooking until the mixture is thick.
It can be served hot or cold. Keep refrigerated.

Yields 2 cups

The Good Egg

Egg Basics	94
Boiled Eggs	94
Poached Eggs	94
Fried Eggs	95
Scrambled Eggs	95
Eggs in Mustard Sauce	96
Egg Salad	97
Upside-down Quiche	98
Spinach and Onion Quiche	99
Wilted Greens	99

Eggs have been maligned for years. They were deemed one of the culprits for raising peoples' cholesterol. Fortunately, recent research has debunked that myth. Nutritionists have now retracted the dire warnings regarding eggs by stating that dietary cholesterol has only a small effect on blood cholesterol levels.

Actually, a balanced diet should include eggs – the whole egg. By using just egg whites, a part of this complete, perfect food is removed. Eggs are an excellent source of high quality protein as well as vitamins and minerals. In addition, Choline in the yolk adds to brain function.

My mother subscribed to that fact. I had a soft-boiled egg for breakfast every morning throughout my school years. I still eat an egg, sometimes two, almost every day and at 70+, my cholesterol level is just fine, thank you. So, please, give eggs a chance to enrich your menus.

And, yes, there is a huge difference between regular and organic eggs. You'll notice that organic eggs have a deeper, darker yellow yolk. They taste better too. So, it's worth paying a little more for organic, farm-fresh eggs.

Egg Basics

Soft Boiled Eggs

Place the eggs in a saucepan to allow them to be covered by at least 1-inch cold water.

When the water is just coming to a boil, tiny bubbles rising to the surface, turn off the heat and wait 2 minutes for very soft, or 3 minutes for soft.

Drain the water immediately and let cold water run over the egg for a minute.

Serve immediately.

Hard Boiled Eggs

Place the eggs in a saucepan to allow them to be covered by at least 1-inch cold water.

When the water is just about to boil – lots of tiny bubbles appearing - turn off the heat and wait 10 minutes or longer.

Drain water from pot and refill with cold water several times, until eggs are totally cooled off.

Remove from the water into a bowl and refrigerate if not using them immediately.

The eggs peel best when done within the hour of cooling.

Poached Eggs

4 inches of water in whatever pan is used
½ cup vinegar
1 teaspoon salt
1 teaspoon vegetable oil
Eggs – amount depending on need – at room temperature

Use a dish large enough to hold several eggs. Eggs should not be crowded.

Bring water mixed with vinegar, oil and salt to a boil. Break an egg into a cup, and then slide the egg from the cup into the simmering water. Bring water back to simmer, then turn off the heat. The top of eggs are opaque in 3 to 5 minutes.

At this point they will be very soft. Cook longer if desired.

Fried Eggs

Eggs at room temperature
1 tablespoon vegetable oil or butter

Make sure to use a pan that can be covered.
A small frying pan is just right for 2 eggs, use a larger one for more.
Heat the oil in the pan over medium heat.
When the butter is foaming add the eggs. Break the eggshell over the pan and slide the egg into it. Repeat with the next one. Turn heat to low and cover the pan. It should take 3 to 5 minutes for the egg whites to be set while the yolks are still soft. At this point they are ready.
If you like them sunny-side up, quickly turn them over for ½ minute. They are done. If you wait any longer everything will be well done.

Favorite Scrambled Eggs

1 tablespoon oil or butter
2 tablespoons pancetta, diced
1 small shallot, diced
4 eggs mixed with 3 tablespoons water or milk
1 tablespoon fresh chives, minced

Heat oil over medium in a frying pan. Add pancetta and sauté until lightly browned.
Add shallots and sauté until softened.
Pour in the beaten eggs and stir after about one minute as eggs are starting to thicken.
Add the chives and keep stirring until eggs are softly set and still have a moist sheen.
Remove from heat and serve immediately.

2 servings

Multiply the recipe as needed.

Eggs in Mustard Sauce

Mashed potatoes or rice make a perfect base for the sauce. A mild vegetable like spring peas or spinach provide a good balance to the spicy sauce.

3 tablespoons unsalted butter
2 tablespoons all-purpose flour
2 tablespoons spicy mustard
½ cup dry white wine
1 to 2 cups water
1 tablespoon lemon juice
Freshly ground pepper
8 eggs, poached

Mashed potatoes or rice for serving

Mustard sauce:
Melt the butter in a medium saucepan. When foaming add the flour and stir until flour just begins to take on a little color. Blend in the mustard and lemon juice. Add wine and 1 cup of water while stirring. Bring slowly to a simmer and add more water until the sauce is medium thick. Simmer over very low heat, stirring occasionally.
Makes approximately 2 cups.

Continue with recipe:
Poach eggs according to directions – page 94. Ideally the yolk will be soft and runny.
Spoon rice or mashed potatoes on individual plates. Lace with a little sauce. Place two eggs strategically in the center and top off with additional sauce.
As the eggs get broken, the slightly runny yolk will mingle with the sauce.
Pass any additional sauce separately.

4 servings

Mustard sauce makes for variety when spooned over fish or vegetables like cauliflower, broccoli or asparagus.

Egg Salad

My friend Louise, from Scotland, and I met for lunch once a month. We would reminisce about our home countries without offending anyone. These lunches turned into playtimes for our children. When our mothers were visiting they were naturally included. One time Louise called to let me know that Greta, her mother, arrived from Scotland, "She is looking forward to your egg salad. I don't know how you're making it, but she likes yours the best."

My mother Edith, who did not speak English, was visiting at the same time. After lunch all of us went for a walk on our country road. Greta and Edith were a few steps ahead. We don't know what they were conversing about, their arms were continually gesturing. They were all smiles when they rejoined us.

12 eggs, hard boiled
3 tablespoons Mayonnaise
2 teaspoons mild mustard
⅛ teaspoon curry powder, optional
Salt and pepper
1 lemon, juiced – possibly more
4 tablespoons chives or young scallions, cut into very thin rounds

Peel all eggs. Using an egg slicer, slice eggs once in each direction and put in a mixing bowl.
In a separate bowl mix the remaining ingredients until smooth. If it is thick, add more lemon juice but the mixture should not be a runny sauce.
Add mixture and chives to eggs and gently fold until all is well blended.

6 to 8 servings

For a dressier presentation, cover a sandwich plate with mixed greens and spoon a serving of egg salad in the center. Decorate with tomato wedges. Serve with rolls or pumpernickel bread slices.

.

Upside-down Quiche

For many years I tried to produce a good bottom crust with a quiche. I finally gave up. I put the crust on top, and that's how I'm still making quiche today. Leek quiche is my favorite. Another is Spinach and Onion quiche.

1 sheet puff pastry, thawed
2 leeks
2 tablespoons vegetable oil
4 eggs
1 cup milk
2 tablespoons all-purpose flour
Salt and pepper
Freshly grated nutmeg

Preheat oven to 375^0F. Grease a 9x9 baking dish or similar size round casserole.
Wash leeks, drain and cut into 1-inch slices, including usable green parts. Heat oil over medium heat in a frying pan and sauté leeks until they start to wilt. Spread the leeks into the bottom of the baking dish. In a small bowl, add milk to the flour while stirring to blend. Then mix in salt, pepper and several scrapes of nutmeg. Pour the mixture over the leeks and slide the dish onto the middle rack of the oven and bake for 15 minutes.
Meanwhile, cut the pastry so that it will fit on top of the egg mixture, making three rows of slits in the top to let moisture escape.
Remove the dish from the oven and quickly fit the pastry on top. Return it to the oven and bake for another 15 - 20 minutes or until the pastry is nicely browned. Remove from the oven to cool.
Cut into quarters and serve crust up or down.

2 servings

To serve 4

Grease a 9x12 baking dish
1 sheet puff pastry
Double all other ingredients and follow the recipe above.
If the pastry sheet does not quite cover the filling, roll it out just enough to fit.
Cut into squares for serving.

Spinach and Onion Quiche

Same quiche recipe as previous, instead of leeks use:

1 large onion, cut in half and sliced thinly
½ pound fresh spinach, rinsed and drained

Sauté the onion until softened, cover with the spinach and stir until it is wilted.
Transfer mixture to the baking dish with a slotted spoon.
Continue according to the quiche recipe.
2 servings

Wilted Greens
A light spring or summer lunch.

4 cups mixed salad greens, torn into bite-size pieces
4 scallions, white and green parts cut into thin diagonal slices
4 tomatoes cut into eighth
Vinaigrette – page 45
Freshly ground pepper
Oil as needed
1 or 2 eggs per person

In a large bowl mix greens and scallions with the vinaigrette and toss well. Divide the greens evenly over 4 dinner plates and sprinkle with freshly ground pepper. Surround greens with the tomatoes.
Heat oil in a large frying pan over medium heat.
Fry eggs over very low heat until the whites are barely set. Center the eggs over each salad plate.
Heat from the eggs will wilt the greens. The runny yolks and vinaigrette combine to a creamy dressing.

4 servings

Gifts from the Sea

Ceviche	101
Easy Shrimp	101
Filet of Sole	102
Grouper	103
Snappers Blues	104

Catch of the day 1974
Derek, Shakti and Jason

Seafood was not on the menu often in land-locked Vermont. But the state's lakes and rivers provided some very tasty fish. Trent came home with the occasional trout or bass after a day of fishing. Whole or filleted, they only took a few minutes in the sauté pan to be ready. Basically it is the same method that is described in the recipe for small snappers, page.

We spent many vacations in Quonochontaug, known simply as Quonnie by the few locals, a small village on the Rhode Island shore. We did get our fill of seafood there. Surf fishing and gathering mussels at low, low tide produced scrumptious dinners.

Lobster, bought – not caught, was always much anticipated. Leftovers turned into a special salad. Everybody loved lobster leftovers!

Ceviche

I was introduced to ceviche during a charter cruise in the Bahamas in 1974. At one couples' cooking turn they made ceviche with the catch of the day.

As the setting set turned sky and ocean fiery red, a debate ensued: Was the fish cooked? Some said yes; others, no.
Regardless, it was delicious.

Scallops are perfectly suited for ceviche. I serve it mostly on special occasions as an appetizer or a main course.

½ pound bay scallops, fresh or frozen
1 lime, juiced – more may be needed - and zest finely grated
1 scallion – sliced thinly on the diagonal
⅛ teaspoon hot pepper flakes

In a serving bowl mix all ingredients, cover and refrigerate. Let the flavors mingle for at least 3 to 4 hours. Some limes do not yield much juice, be sure scallops are covered.

4 appetizer servings

When multiplying the amounts, a container of lime juice from the store may be more efficient.

Easy - Saucy Shrimp
It doesn't get easier than this.

Shrimp* - amounts depend on servings; cleaned if fresh
Best quality salsa - or make your own
Fresh cilantro, chopped for serving

Put shrimp in a saucepan, barely cover it with salsa.
Heat over medium until shrimp is completely opaque. It only takes a few minutes once the salsa starts bubbling.
Serve immediately over rice, dust with cilantro.

(* Fresh or frozen - works equally well - only the cooking time differs. The key is not to overcook the shrimp.)

Baked Fillet of Sole

Sole is a mild fish, a change from heavier, heartier types. I did not eat fish until well into adulthood, then I learned to love this fillet dish and serve it often.

1 tablespoon unsalted butter
4 shallots, diced
2 tablespoons unsalted butter
4 fillets of sole, thawed if frozen
Salt
½ cup breadcrumbs
1 lemon, juiced
2 tablespoons unsalted butter, cut into small nuggets
¾ cup dry white wine
1 cup white mushrooms, cut into small dice
2 tablespoons fresh Italian parsley, minced

Preheat oven to 350F.
Sauté shallots in 1 tablespoon butter over medium heat. Set aside.
Put 2 tablespoons butter in a Pyrex baking dish. Place in oven and let brown.
Lightly salt fish fillets and dredge both sides in breadcrumbs
Remove dish from oven. Scrape shallots into dish and spread evenly. Place fish fillets in one layer on top. Sprinkle lemon juice over fish and scatter butter nuggets on top. Pour wine around sides and bake for 20 minutes.
Meanwhile mix mushrooms and parsley.
Top fillets with the mushroom mixture and bake for another 10 minutes.
Remove fish fillets with a spatula onto serving plates.

4 servings

Baked Grouper

Absolutely delicious when going from the ocean into the oven within hours. Grouper is an oily fish and does not need additional fats.

Oil for greasing the pan
1 grouper fillet, use 2 if small
1 lemon, juiced
Freshly ground pepper
1 large onion, cut into very thin rounds
2 tomatoes, also sliced into thin rounds
½ cup dry white wine
2 tablespoons fresh parsley, minced
8 lemon wedges

Preheat oven to 375F. Grease baking dish, set aside.
Put fish into baking dish and sprinkle with lemon juice and ground pepper. Cover fish entirely with onion slices and top those with tomato slices, leaving as few gaps as possible. Pour wine into the dish.
Bake in the middle of the oven for 30 minutes. Fillets are done when flakes are easily separated when poked with a fork.
Remove from oven and sprinkle with parsley. Cut into serving sizes and serve. Drizzle with pan juices.
Pass lemon wedges around in a separate dish.

4 servings

Snapper Blues

Snapper blue is a young grouper, mostly caught in small streams running towards the ocean.

When vacationing on Rhode Island's shore, we found several rivulets where the children would get their catch of the day. Then we headed home and immediately prepped them for the frying pan.

There would be nothing tastier that day!

Basic method:
Snappers
Salt and pepper
Breadcrumbs
Vegetable oil

Rinse the snappers that have been cleaned out and the head removed. Heat oil over medium heat in a sizable frying pan to hold several snappers at one time.
Coat each fish with breadcrumbs. Fry on one side until golden brown, approximately 5 minutes. Turn fish over to brown the other side.
Serve with wedges of lemon on the side.

The same method can be used for trout and other fresh fish.

Things with Wings

Coq au Vin	106
Chicken Cacciatore	107
Chicken Flambé	108
Chicken Paprika	109
Chicken Salad Tarragon	110
Duck Breast	111
Favorite Goose	112
Five-Spice Chicken	113
Yogurt Sauce	113
Grilled Chicken	114
Roasted Chicken	115
Thai Chicken	116

When I was growing up in postwar Berlin, chicken was extremely expensive, served only at special occasions. Sometimes a year would pass before we had a chicken dinner again.

Now I love to prepare chicken as often as possible, always looking for different recipes.

When we raised chickens in Vermont, I became aware of the taste difference versus store bought. Especially when roasting a whole chicken. Farm-raised fowl has less fat under the skin, but what flavor!

Luckily, farm-raised, free-range chickens are available at most butcher counters today.

Coq au Vin

How could I not include an adaptation of this classic? I especially remember a luncheon in Provence. We were tracing Cezanne's footsteps in Le Tholonet and then recovered in a bistro with a savory coq au vin and a glass of their red house wine. I try to recreate those flavors when making coq au vin.

¼ pound sliced bacon
1 3 to 4 pound chicken, cut into 10 serving pieces
Salt as needed
1 tablespoon vegetable oil
1 carrot, diced
4 medium onions, quartered
2 garlic cloves, minced
1 teaspoon sumac (optional)*
2 tablespoon all purpose flour
2 tomatoes, diced
2 cups dry red or white wine
1 cup chicken or veggie broth
1 teaspoon dried thyme (1 tablespoon if fresh, minced)
1 bay leaf
1 pound medium sized white mushrooms, quartered
Freshly ground pepper to taste
2 tablespoons minced fresh parsley

In a Dutch oven render the bacon fat, remove bacon and save.
Dry the chicken pieces, dust with salt and sauté in the bacon fat until lightly browned. Remove and set aside.
Heat the oil, add onions and carrots and sauté until softened, about 10 minutes. Add garlic and sumac and stir until fragrant.
Blend the flour into the mixture, add tomatoes and wine, bring to a simmer while stirring and scraping off any browned bits.
Return chicken and crumbled bacon and heat thoroughly. Add chicken broth, bay leaf and thyme and bring to a simmer again. Cover and reduce heat to a low simmer.
After 20 minutes turn chicken pieces over and add mushrooms, pepper and parsley. Continue to simmer for an additional 30 minutes or until chicken pieces are done.
Adjust seasonings and serve.
4 to 6 servings
(* A nod to an interesting cooking class in Amman, Jordan.)

Chicken Cacciatore

Whenever I asked the family, "What should I make with this chicken?" "Cacciatore!" was the unanimous feedback.

1 3 to 4 pound chicken cut into 10 serving pieces, or any combo of breast, leg and thigh
Salt and pepper
2 tablespoons vegetable oil
2 ounces pancetta, diced
1 large onion, coarsely chopped
2 green peppers, chopped
1 large clove garlic, diced
2 cups tomatoes, quartered
1 cup dry white wine
1 tablespoon fresh oregano
1 tablespoon fresh basil
½ pound white mushrooms, sliced
Minced fresh parsley to sprinkle over top when serving

In a large pot brown chicken pieces on all sides in the oil. Dust with salt and pepper. Remove from pot.
Add pancetta and fry until it starts to crisp, then add onion and green peppers and sauté until onion start to soften. Push to the sides, add garlic and stir for a minute. Mix into the onion and pepper mass. Add tomatoes and wine, bring slowly to a boil. Add herbs and blend.
Return chicken to the pot, cover and simmer for 20 minutes. Add mushrooms and continue cooking until chicken is done, about another 20 minutes.
Keep in mind that breast pieces are done sooner than other parts. Remove them when ready and return to the sauce before serving.
Adjust seasonings if needed.

4 to 6 servings

Poulet Flambé

I adapted chicken with brandy sauce from a bistro cookbook, *Art of Simple French Cookery* by Alexander Watt, Rasher Verlag, 1961. The book with recipes of some of my favorites was a farewell present when I left Basel to come to New York.

The recipe can easily be made in larger amounts and was one of the favorites at Ski Club 10 in Sugarbush, Vermont, when I was chef there.

1 tablespoon vegetable oil or butter
1 3 to 4 pound chicken, cut into 10 serving pieces or buy cut-up pieces
½ cup dry white wine, maybe more
2 tablespoons brandy
1 cup heavy cream (sour cream can be substituted)
Salt and pepper to taste

Rub chicken with salt and pepper and quickly brown in oil on all sides in a Dutch oven over medium heat.
Add wine, cover, and simmer until almost done, approximately 45 minutes.
Uncover. Increase heat and pour previously warmed brandy over the chicken and quickly hold lighted match close to chicken. A large flame will quickly burn out.

Be sure to do this on a kitchen counter or table where nothing flammable is near.

Remove chicken and keep warm.
Add cream to the pan and bring to a boil while gently stirring. Lower heat and simmer until sauce is slightly thickened. Adjust seasonings to taste.
Serve while hot.

4 servings

Best served with rice, a good base for the delicate sauce.

Chicken Paprika

Chicken Paprika is a welcome change from grilled meats. Hungarian paprika, available in specialty stores, gives a deeper flavor. It is easy to make ahead when expecting company. Just reheat when the time is right.

1 3 to 4 pound chicken, separated into 10 serving pieces; or any combination of assorted cuts
2 tablespoons vegetable oil
1 large onion, halved and sliced very thin
Salt and pepper
2 tablespoons Hungarian paprika
1 cup dry red wine
1 tablespoon tomato paste
½ cup sour cream

Heat the oil in a Dutch oven and brown chicken on all sides. Push meat to sides and sauté the onion until translucent. Mix the paprika with the onions and sauté for a couple of minutes. Add the wine, tomato paste, salt and pepper. Mix all together and bring to a boil. Reduce heat to very low, cover and simmer for 40 to 45 minutes, until chicken is done.
Take a little juice from the pot and blend with the sour cream in a little bowl, enough to thin the sour cream and add mixture to the sauce. Slowly bring mixture to simmer.
Serve over rice or noodles.

4 to 5 servings

Chicken Salad Tarragon

This was one of the choices at a buffet dinner at our daughter Shakti's wedding eve party. It was June and we could host family and friends in our backyard. The salad is simple to make ahead and in large amounts, assuring to have plenty for seconds and thirds. The crowd of hearty eaters did my preparations justice.

Use only the best and freshest ingredients available, including organic chicken, for simply delicious results.

4 boneless chicken breasts
1 cup yogurt, drained
½ cup heavy cream
¼ cup mayonnaise
2 celery ribs, cut into thinly crosswise
4 artichoke hearts, cut into eighth
1 tablespoon minced fresh tarragon
Salt and freshly ground pepper to taste

Preheat oven to 350F.
Arrange chicken in a baking pan and cover with yogurt. Bake for 20 minutes, 25 if breasts are large. Remove and set aside to cool.
Take chicken out of the dish, with some yogurt left on the meat, and shred chicken* into bite size chunks.
Mix cream and mayo well, pour over chicken, add celery and tarragon, mix again.
Add artichoke hearts, salt and pepper and gently blend into the mixture.
Cover and refrigerate for a minimum of 4 hours.
Taste again before serving.

*Do shred instead of cutting, for a more attractive presentation.

4 to 6 servings

The recipe can be prepared and refrigerated 1 day before serving. For a better taste experience, remove the dish from the refrigerator an hour before serving to take off the chill.

Duck Breast

A simple alternative to a whole duck. Look for packages of smaller duck breasts at Whole Foods. Each package contains two individually wrapped pieces. Ideal for single servings or a perfect dinner for 2.

4 frozen duck breasts – 2 per package
2 shallots, minced
Pinch of salt
1 cup dark cherries, thawed if frozen
¾ cup red wine
Salt and pepper to taste

Sauté breast in a frying pan according to directions on package, approximately 15 minutes. Remove from pan to a plate and cover.
Remove all but 1 tablespoon fat renderings, add shallots and sauté over low heat until soft, about 5 minutes.
Add wine, scraping juices off the bottom and simmer for 10 minutes. Add cherries and cook another 2 minutes.
Place 1 breast on each plate, sauce meat and arrange shallots and cherries around each.
Serve with potato dumplings or gnocchi.

4 servings

Favorite New Year's Goose
Simply delicious. It is a no fuss holiday recipe.

1 goose, generally 5 to 6 pounds, thawed if frozen
1 large apple, cored and diced
¾ cup prunes, diced
1 tablespoon all-purpose flour
Salt and pepper
Giblet broth as needed

Cook giblet broth – see **Basic Broth**, page 20

Preheat oven to 350F.
Rub duck with salt inside and out.
Mix apples and prunes and stuff loosely into cavity. Close opening with toothpicks. Truss legs close to body with butcher twine. Prick fatty areas all over with a sharp tool to let fat drip out while roasting.
Put goose breast side down on a rack in roasting pan and place in middle of oven.
After 1 hour turn goose over. Roast another hour.
Turn heat to 425F for 15 minutes. When bird looks browned and 'pop-up' is up, remove duck. Total roasting time is approximately a little over 2 hours.
Transfer goose to platter, cover with foil and let rest 15 to 30 minutes.
Pour almost all accumulated fat into a storage dish.
Scrape remainder into a saucepan. Add flour and stir over low heat until well blended. Turn up heat if more color is desired. Stirring gently, add ½ cup of broth at a time. Bring to boil each time until gravy reaches consistency of heavy cream.
Spoon the stuffing into a small bowl.
Cut goose into serving pieces and serve.

3 to 4 servings

Five-Spice Chicken
Tender, juicy and delicious with deep flavor

2 tablespoons soy sauce
4 tablespoons lime juice
1½ tablespoons cumin
1 tablespoon coriander
4 large garlic cloves, minced
½ teaspoon red pepper flakes
¼ teaspoon cinnamon
4 ginger slices, julienned
1 tablespoon vegetable oil
4 skinless chicken breast halves*
2 tablespoons vegetable oil

Combine first nine ingredients in a shallow dish. Add chicken, turn to coat and let marinade for a minimum of 30 minutes. Turn a couple of times if possible.

Heat oil in a frying pan to medium. Take chicken from dish, leaving marinade on the meat. Sauté breasts for approximately 6 minutes on each side or until fork tender. Chicken should be well browned, spices not burnt.

Top each chicken breast with a spoonful of yogurt sauce and pass the remainder in a separate bowl.

4 servings
(*Can be made with any combination of chicken parts as well.)

Yogurt Sauce

Besides being the perfect sauce for this chicken dish, yogurt sauce goes well with any spicy foods and also makes an excellent dip.

1 cup plain yogurt, drained of excess liquid
1 garlic clove, crushed
2 tablespoon cilantro chopped
3 tablespoons lime juice

Mix yogurt and lime juice and stir until smooth. Add cilantro and blend.

Grilled Chicken

The dressing is one of my favorite for grilling chicken. The combination of sweet and tart especially suits chicken.

For a spicier version I use the Five-Spice Chicken marinade from the previous recipe. It brings tasty results every time.

10 assorted chicken parts – breasts cut in half, drumsticks and thighs
2 tablespoon vegetable oil
2 tablespoons lemon juice
2 tablespoons maple syrup
⅛ teaspoon salt
½ teaspoon red pepper flakes

Preheat the grill.
In a small bowl mix oil, lemon juice, maple syrup, salt and pepper flakes.
Brush chicken pieces on all sides and put them skin-side down on the hot grill. Reduce heat to medium and grill for 5 minutes.
Brush chicken pieces and turn them over, grilling another 5 minutes.
Turn heat to low and continue grilling for 10 minutes.
Brush chicken with sauce and turn pieces over and grill for another 10 minutes or until chicken is done.
Breast pieces are done sooner, so keep checking.

4 to 6 servings

Oven Roasted Chicken

There is nothing like a chicken roasting in the oven. The aroma permeating the kitchen creates a Thanksgiving-like anticipation. Once in the oven it takes care of itself.

Kitchen shears help when it comes to carving but a heavy kitchen knife can also separate the backbone from the other parts.

Derek, our youngest, was five when he first tackled roasting a whole chicken, his absolute favorite. He learned to maneuver the poultry shears and proudly brought the platter with the cut-up chicken to the table.

1 whole chicken, 3 to 4 pounds
Vegetable oil
2 tablespoons dried tarragon*, crumbled
Salt and pepper
1 lemon, cut in half
Oil for greasing roasting pan if used

Preheat oven to 325^0F. Grease the bottom of a roasting pan if not using a roasting rack.
Tuck the wings under the chicken. Take any extra fat out of the chicken's cavity. Loosen the skin over the breast and slide the fat under both sides as far as you can. Gently rub oil all over the outside. Then rub a little salt and pepper over the skin followed by rubbing tarragon over all sides also. Take a little tarragon and slide between skin and breast meat. Sprinkle any remaining tarragon into the cavity along with the lemon halves.
Pull the skin over the cavity and secure with a couple of toothpicks.
Bake for 1 hour and 15 minutes. Remove the pan from the oven and cover the chicken lightly with foil. Let sit for at least 15 minutes.
Remove the toothpicks and any remaining fat that was stuffed under the skin before carving.

4 to 5 servings

(* I prefer dried tarragon for its more intense flavor. Rosemary is a tasty alternative.)

Thai Chicken

From forays into Asian cuisine, this emerged as a favorite. Do not overcook the chicken or snow peas for best results.

2 chicken breast halves, cut into bite-size pieces
1 14-ounce can unsweetened coconut milk
2 tablespoons green curry paste
1 teaspoon grated fresh ginger
2 garlic cloves, peeled and halved
2 tablespoons lime juice
1 small fresh red chili, seeded and thinly julienned
½ pound fresh snow peas
10 fresh basil leaves, torn into small pieces

Clean snow peas and set aside.
In a large saucepan bring the coconut milk and curry paste to simmer. Add the chicken and simmer for 5 minutes.
Add ginger, garlic, lime juice and chilies and simmer an additional 3 minutes.
Add snow peas and simmer for a few minutes. They are basically getting blanched and should still be crunchy.
Remove garlic pieces, add basil leaves, stir and serve immediately over rice.

4 servings

All About Beef

Beef Ragout Country Style	119
Beef and Beer	120
Beef Salad	121
Königsberger Klopse	122
Braised Cuts	124
Beef Short Ribs	124
Oxtail Ragout	124
Hockey Chili	125
Vegetarian Chili	126
Hungarian Goulash	126
Liver – Berlin Style	127
Stuffed Cabbage	128
Meat Loaf	130
Pot Roast	131
Rouladen	132
Spanish Rice	133

Beef was always special. My mother cooked mostly economy cuts like oxtail, ground beef and stewing beef.

I continued to make the same kind of dishes for my family. After living in the U.S. for a while, I started to appreciate roast beef and porterhouse steaks. They became my standard order in restaurants. I can't believe I finished the large servings that were on the plate.

Today my beef cravings are satisfied with half a serving, or even less, of a rib eye steak. The steak just needs a dusting of salt on both sides and a rub of coarsely ground pepper into the sides. Then let it sit at room temperature for an hour before sautéing in a cast iron pan to your preferred doneness. I like beef rare. Any leftovers will be a delicious addition to salad plate another day.

I love the aroma that fills the air when slow cooking a stew or pot roast. And I also love the fact that these dishes can be cooked at my leisure, way ahead of dinner time. That way, when we have company I can spend more time with our friends and not be stressing in the kitchen.

Buy the best beef you can. Avoid light pink colored cuts, indicating insufficient aging. When I need cubed meat I buy chuck roasts, then cut the meat into the desired size chunks. This is the only way to know for sure what cut you are cooking.

This rule applies equally to pork, lamb or veal.

Beef Ragout Country Style

Representing Vermont, I cooked this simple, never fail recipe, at the National Beef Cook-Off in 1986, in Detroit.

Discerning judges awarded my ragout second place. After the awards ceremony I was told, "...the beef was cooked perfectly, moist and tender, the best of all entries." That was good enough for me. The judge continued, "We had a tie for first place for over an hour. Finally Hot Hunan Hoagies won because it was fitting the emerging trend for convenience."

Hot Hunan Hoagies was sautéed beef served in a bun.

Who knows what might have happened had I piled my beef into a pita pocket?

2 pounds chuck roast, cut into 1 ¼-inch cubes
2 tablespoons vegetable oil
3 large onions cut into eight chunks each
4 large garlic cloves, minced
1 teaspoon dried thyme
3 tablespoons fresh Italian parsley, chopped
⅛ teaspoon salt and freshly ground pepper each
1 28-ounce can peeled tomatoes, drained and quartered
1 cup dry red wine – more if needed
½ cup beef broth
½ pound white mushrooms, quartered
1 small can black olives
2 tablespoons fresh parsley, chopped

Heat the oil in a large Dutch oven and sear the meat. Do not crowd, do in batches if necessary,
Add onions, stir and brown lightly. Then push mixture to sides and add garlic to bottom of pot. Stir garlic for a minute to bring out flavor. Add tomatoes, thyme, salt, pepper and three tablespoons parsley and mix. Add wine and just enough broth to cover everything and bring to a boil. Cover, reduce heat and simmer for 1 hour.*
Add mushrooms and simmer another 30 minutes, or until beef is tender.
Adjust seasonings, add olives, remaining parsley and reheat.

4-6 servings
(*Can be cooked several days in advance to this point.)

Beef and Beer

A Belgian recipe given to me by a friend from Brugge.

3 pounds chuck roast, cut into 1-inch cubes
2 tablespoons vegetable oil
6 cups onions, halved and thinly sliced
Salt and pepper
6 garlic cloves, minced
3 cups beer
6 sprigs fresh parsley, 1 bay leaf, 1 teaspoon dried thyme
2 tablespoons cornstarch mixed with
2 tablespoons vinegar

Heat the oil in a large Dutch oven and brown the beef on all side. Best done in batches so that the meat is not crowded and browns better. Remove meat to a platter and sprinkle lightly with salt.
Add the onions to the pot and brown them over medium heat. Add more oil if needed.
When the onions are brown, add salt and pepper and push them to the sides of the pot. Add the garlic and stir or a minute until it is fragrant. Mix garlic and onions.
Return the beef to the pot and blend into the onions.
Add the beer and bring to a boil. Add the parsley springs, bay leaf and thyme. Cover and simmer over very low heat for 1 hour. Taste the sauce and add salt if needed.
Simmer for another ½ hour and the beef should then be fork tender.
Remove parsley and bay leaf.
Stir the cornstarch mixture into the sauce. When it is simmering remove from the heat and serve.

6 servings

Beef Salad

My favorite picnic salad. Meat, vegetables and dressing easily keep in a cooler and get mixed on the spot.

1 small flank steak*
4 cups asparagus, sliced diagonally into 2-inch pieces
1 bunch broccoli, cut into bite-size florets
1 cup fresh snow peas

Grill or broil flank steak to desired doneness. Set aside to cool.
In lightly salted boiling water, blanch asparagus for 30 seconds. Remove with slotted spoon into bowl with cold water. Drain and set aside.
Add broccoli to same water and blanch for 30 seconds. Remove with slotted spoon into bowl with cold water. Drain and set aside.
Blanch snow peas following the same procedure.
Transfer veggies to a bowl and keep in the refrigerator.
Slice meat into bite size thin slices across the grain and refrigerate.
When ready to serve toss beef slices with the dressing until well coated. Add vegetables and gently toss again.
Best served at room temperature.

4 to 6 servings

*Store-bought prepared roast beef can be substituted. Buy a 1-inch slab and slice into thin slices, like a steak.

Ginger Dressing

⅓ cup soy sauce
¼ cup apple cider vinegar
3 tablespoon sesame oil, olive oil can be substituted
1 ½-inch piece fresh ginger, peeled and grated
¼ teaspoon sugar
Freshly ground pepper

Combine all ingredients for the dressing.

Königsberger Klopse

Königsberger Klopse is a traditional meatball dish in my hometown, Berlin.

Originally, klopse are about 3-inches in diameter. I've always made them smaller. They cook faster, flavors permeate the meat better and these meatballs stay moister.

This dish was one of the courses at the state dinner for President Obama when he visited Berlin in June 2013. Königsberger Klopse was served with pureed beets and mashed potatoes.

The recipe also works very well as a warm buffet dish when entertaining a crowd.

1 pound ground chuck or veal, or half and half
1 small onion, finely minced or grated
1 egg
½ cup plain breadcrumbs
Salt and pepper to taste

Broth
4 cups water
½ teaspoon salt
2 bay leaves
10 juniper berries
20 peppercorns
5 cloves

Sauce
1 tablespoons unsalted butter
1 tablespoon vegetable oil
2 tablespoons all-purpose flour
1½ to 2 cups veggie or chicken broth
2 tablespoons sour cream
½ lemon, juiced
2 tablespoons capers
1 small dill pickle, finely diced

Mix the first 5 ingredients well, add a bit of water if it seems dry. Form mass into balls about 1½-inches in diameter. (1-inch for a buffet.)

In a stew pot combine water, herbs and salt and simmer for 5 to 10 minutes. Add meatballs and poach them for 10 minutes. Remove meatballs and let the broth cool off.

In a sauce pan blend oil and butter over medium heat. Add flour and stir for 3 to 5 minutes but do not let mixture get brown.

Strain some of the cooled broth into the mixture and bring to a boil while stirring. Add more liquid as the sauce thickens. Just as it starts to simmer add the sour cream, lemon juice, capers and pickles. Consistency of heavy cream is the goal. Let sauce simmer for 10 minutes.

Return klopse to the sauce and simmer another 10 minutes.

Taste to correct seasoning and serve.

Ideally served over mashed potatoes or rice.

4 servings

The recipe multiplies easily.

Braised Cuts of Beef

Oxtail and short ribs get tenderized by a slow braise in red wine. If you never had oxtail, do try. It is rich in flavor. Look for the widest rounds of oxtail with a good portion of meat.

When buying short ribs, choose meaty ones. The same goes for lamb shanks – I'm sneaking lamb in here because of the cooking method.

All are braised similar to the oxtail recipe below.

Oxtail Ragout

2 to 3 pounds oxtail, usually already cut into thick slices
Salt and pepper
2 tablespoons vegetable oil
3 tablespoons pancetta, diced
2 onions, chopped
2 carrots, diced
2 stalks celery, diced
1 cup dry red wine
1 cup veggie broth
8 Peppercorns, crushed
2 bay leaves
½ cup sour cream (optional)

Rub a little salt and pepper into all sides of the oxtail slices.
Heat the oil in a Dutch oven and brown the oxtail on all sides. Add the vegetables and sauté them for a few minutes. Pour the wine into the pot and let it come to a boil. Add just enough broth to barely cover the meat. Set the rest aside.
Add peppercorns and bay leaf and when boiling, lower the heat, cover and simmer for about 2 hours or until the meat separates from the bones easily. Check from time to time in case more liquid is needed.
Add the sour cream, if using, taste and adjust seasonings.

4 servings

When braising **short ribs** or **lamb shanks,** do not add sour cream to finish off the sauce.

Hockey Chili

We were an ice hockey family. Three, four or more afternoons were spent at hockey rinks, often at several locations. Trent was coaching and I was the hockey mom, trying to have a warm meal waiting for all. On Sundays I cooked several dishes to be reheated as needed. Chili was a popular staple.

A most satisfying cold weather dinner after whatever is keeping you out in the cold.

1 pound kidney beans, soaked overnight and drained
3 tablespoons vegetable oil
1 pound ground chuck
1 large onion, chopped
2 carrots, diced
1 green pepper, chopped
2 celery stalks, diced
3 cloves garlic, minced
1 28-ounce can Roma tomatoes, diced, juice reserved
1 small can green chile pepper, drained and coarsely chopped
1 cup dry red wine
2 tablespoons chili powder
1 teaspoon red pepper flakes
Salt and pepper to taste

In large stew pot heat oil over medium heat, add chuck and brown while breaking it into small crumbs.

When meat is browned push it to sides, add onions, green pepper and celery and sauté until they start to soften. Add garlic and stir for a minute, do not let it get brown. Add tomatoes, red wine, green chile, chili powder and pepper flakes. Mix well, add beans and bring to a gentle boil. Lower heat, cover and simmer for 1 hour or until beans are tender.

During cooking add reserved tomato juice and more wine if chili seems dry.

Taste and add salt and pepper and more chili if preferred.

8 servings

The recipe easily is doubled or cut in half.

Vegetarian Chili
You'll never miss the meat.

Same recipe as above except:
Omit ground chuck and start with sautéing the vegetables.
Double the amounts of all vegetables.
Proceed with the recipe as described above.

Pass grated parmesan cheese separately.

8 servings

Hungarian Goulash
Long cooking at low temperatures is the 'secret' to a good goulash. When finished, the onions should be disintegrated, making a thick, rich sauce.

1 pounds beef chuck, cut into 2-inch cubes
1 pound pork shoulder, cut into 2-ich cubes
2 tablespoons vegetable oil
4 large onions, minced
4 large cloves garlic, crushed
4 tablespoons Hungarian paprika
2 teaspoons grated lemon rind
1 tablespoon tomato paste
½ cup dry red wine, more if needed
2 green peppers, julienned
Salt to taste
1 large sour pickle, chopped

Heat oil in Dutch oven to medium. Add beef and onions, mix well, cover and simmer for 10 minutes.
Add garlic, paprika, cumin, lemon rind, tomato paste and wine. Cook for 2 hours over low heat, it should barely simmer.
Add green peppers mix well, simmer for an additional ½ hour or until meat is fork tender and the sauce dark and thick.
Sprinkle chopped pickle over each serving.

6 to 8 servings

Gebratene Leber
Liver Berlin Style

The apples-and-onion combination is a Berlin specialty. I love the savory flavor and also use it for a pork filet recipe.

In the spring of 2014 I visited family in Berlin. Every restaurant featured their version of *Gebratene Leber*. On a rare, mild day in early April my sister Margot, cousin Hannelore and I drove through the Grunewald Forest to a restaurant on the banks of the Havel River. Sitting at an outdoor table overlooking the calm water, we enjoyed our plates of tender liver served with the traditional fluffy mashed potatoes.

2 tablespoons vegetable oil
2 large onions, halved and sliced thinly
2 golden delicious apples, peeled, cored and cut into ½-inch wedges
1 pound organic beef liver slices, ½-inch thick
2 tablespoons unsalted butter or more if needed
Salt and pepper

2 frying pans

Heat oil in one frying pan and sauté onions. When they are starting to take on color, push onions to the side of the pan and add the apples. When the apples turn lightly brown on one side, turn them over to brown the other side.
All along keep stirring the onions so that they brown, but not burn.
When the apple/onion mixture is done, turn off the heat and cover to keep warm.
Heat butter in the second frying pan. Dry the liver slices with a paper towel and pat salt and pepper into both sides. Place livers in the butter and brown over medium-high on one side - do not crowd the liver slices. Fry them in several batches if needed).
This should not take more than 2 or 3 minutes. Turn them over and brown the other side. Remove when juice is pink when pricked with a skewer.
Top liver slices with apple wedges and browned onions. Drizzle some of the pan juices over the traditional mashed potatoes.

4 servings

Kohlrouladen

Stuffed Cabbage is a very traditional German main dish, varying from region to region.

It takes a couple of separate steps to prepare, so it is best done ahead of time, if possible the day before. You can then just reheat the cabbage rolls when needed.

1 medium savoy cabbage
½ pound ground beef
½ pound ground pork
1 small onion, minced
1 egg
½ cup breadcrumbs
Salt and pepper
2 tablespoons fresh parsley, minced
2 slices bacon, diced
2 tablespoons vegetable oil
¼ cup veggie broth
½ cup dry white wine
1 tablespoon cornstarch mixed with a little water to make a paste

Kitchen twine or toothpicks to secure cabbage rolls

Bring water to a boil in a large pot.
Meanwhile remove the core from the bottom of the cabbage with a sharp knife. Submerge the cabbage in the boiling water for about 10 minutes. Remove it and set aside to cool.
When the cabbage is cool enough to handle remove the outer leaves, one at a time, until you have 12 leaves. You may need more if some leaves are small; in that case you need to combine 2 leaves for 1 cabbage roll.
Combine beef, pork, onion, egg, breadcrumbs, parsley salt and pepper to a meatloaf like mixture.

Assembly:
Divide meat mixture into 12 balls. Put one cabbage leaf on a board with the widest part closest to you. Take one meat ball and form it into a tight roll. Place the roll on the wide end of the cabbage leaf. Grab the bottom of the leaf and fold over the meat and roll one turn. Fold both sides of the cabbage over the roll
and continue rolling the cabbage until it is a tight package. Secure the end with a toothpick or twine.
Repeat until all 12 rolls are done.
Heat a Dutch oven over medium heat and fry the bacon until brown but not burnt. Add the oil and when it is heated, lightly brown the cabbage rolls on all sides. This may be done in batches for easier handling.
When they are done, return all to the pot and add the broth and wine. Bring the sauce to a boil, reduce heat, cover the pot and simmer for about 45 minutes.
Remove cabbage rolls to a platter.
While the sauce is simmering add the cornstarch and simmer until the sauce is opaque. Do not boil again.

6 servings

Meat Loaf

I always loved meat loaf, but not the greasy gravy that usually was served.

So, instead of making gravy I serve mushroom sauce or a quick tomato sauce with meat loaf.

1 pound ground chuck
1 pound ground pork
1 egg
1 large onion, minced
½ teaspoon salt
½ teaspoon freshly ground pepper
2 tablespoons dried thyme, or any combination of thyme, marjoram and tarragon
1 cup fine breadcrumbs
Water for mixing
Oil to prepare the baking dish

Preheat oven to 325º. Lightly grease bottom of a 6x9 Pyrex baking dish, or similar vessel.
In a bowl mix the first 9 ingredients. It is best to use your hands for thorough distribution. Form an oblong loaf about 2-inches high. Place in center of prepared dish.
Bake for 1 hour and 15 minutes.
Remove meat loaf from dish onto a serving platter, cover with foil to keep warm.

6 to 8 servings

Meat Loaf Variation

When I cannot get ground pork, I use:
1 pound sweet Italian sausage instead.
Squeeze the sausage out of the casings and proceed with the recipe above.
Omit herbs and add 1 teaspoon ground fennel instead

Heidi's Pot Roast

Sauerbraten is not a favorite of mine. I much prefer pot roast and make it often.

3 to 4 pounds chuck roast
2 tablespoons vegetable oil
2 thick slices bacon
2 onions, chopped
4 tomatoes, quartered
2 cups dry red wine
Salt and pepper
2 branches fresh thyme, crushed
4 carrots, peeled and cut into 1-inch length
3 leek stalks, washed and cut into 1-inch slices
1 celery stalk, cut into ½-inch slices
2 tablespoons all-purpose flour
½ cup cold water or beef broth

Heat oil in Dutch oven, brown the bacon and then add the roast and brown on all sides.
Add onions and sauté until translucent. Add tomatoes, salt and pepper and mix with onions. Add wine and thyme and bring to a boil. Cover and turn heat down to a low simmer.
After 2 hours, turn up the heat and add remaining vegetables. When simmering again, cover and lower heat. Cook for an additional hour. Remove meat and keep warm.
Mix flour and water and add to the liquid in the pot. Bring to a boil while stirring. Simmer for additional 10 minutes. Taste and adjust seasonings.
Remove vegetables and sauce to separate dishes.
Cut meat against the grain into serving slices, place them on platter and dinner is ready.

4 to 6 servings plus more for the next day

Rouladen

A traditional German dish, usually served with potato dumplings and red cabbage. Preparing Rouladen involves several steps and they are often made in advance. Besides, reheating always improves flavors.

8 slices top round, sliced as thin as possible by a butcher
½ cup mustard
8 thin strips of bacon (buy a chunk if possible)
1 med onion, julienned
2 dill pickles, julienned
Kitchen twine
Salt
4 tablespoons vegetable oil
1 medium onion, quartered
1 large carrot, quartered
3 tablespoons all-purpose flour
½ cup beef broth
1 cup dry red wine – more if needed
1 teaspoon tomato paste
1 bay leaf
2 teaspoons dried marjoram
Ground pepper to taste

Spread 1 tablespoon mustard on a slice of beef. At the narrow end place strips of bacon, several pieces each of pickle and onion. Roll the beef, tucking the sides in, into a tight roll. Secure with twine or thin metal skewers. Repeat with remaining beef slices. Sprinkle each lightly with salt.
Heat oil in a Dutch oven to medium. Sauté the beef rolls until brown on all sides. Set rouladen aside.
Add onion and carrots to pot and sauté until lightly browned. Add flour and whisk until it takes on color. Add broth while stirring and scraping up any stuck parts, add wine and bring to a boil. Sauce should not be too thin. Add tomato paste, bay leaf, marjoram and freshly ground pepper to taste. Bring to boil again. Return rouladen to pot, bring to boil again. Turn heat low, cover and simmer for 1 hour.
Remove string or skewers from rouladen. Blend veggies into the gravy, when smooth return rouladen, reheat and serve.

8 servings

Spanish Rice

This is one of our daughter Shakti's favorite meals. She asked to cook it herself when she was seven. Can you guess that it is easy?

1 tablespoon vegetable oil
1 pound ground beef
1 onion, diced
2 green peppers, diced
1 cup Uncle Ben's rice
1 cup crushed tomatoes
2 ½ cups water
1 beef bouillon cube – dissolved in the water
1 tablespoon soy sauce
Salt and pepper to taste

Grated parmesan for serving

In a large skillet heat coco butter over medium heat and brown beef. Push beef aside, add onion and green pepper and sauté for 5 minutes or until vegetables are fragrant.
Add rice, tomatoes, water with dissolved bouillon cube and soy sauce. Stir well, bring mixture to a boil, reduce heat and cover. Simmer over low heat for about 25 minutes or until all moisture is absorbed. Adjust seasoning if needed.
Serve with grated parmesan.

4 to 6 servings

Although I use brown or basmati rice most often, for this recipe Uncle Ben's works best.

Lamb

Butterflied Leg of Lamb	135
Curried Lamb	136
Lamb with Dill	137
Lamb and Onion Stew	138
Roast Leg of Lamb	139
Lamb Salad	140
Lamb and Green Beans Stew	142

Photo by Derek Smith

For over twenty years we raised sheep, as well as other critters on our farm in Vermont. I could write a book just about lamb and mutton cooking. Here I'm including our absolute favorite recipes.

Actually, we preferred the bit more mature meat of the one-year old ewe, over true lamb that is just two or three months old. First of all the carcass weighs more, providing more meat and the flavor is gamier, which we liked. Being grass fed, our lamb also had less fat than commercial cuts.

I substituted lamb in beef recipes with wonderful results: meat loaf; ground lamb rolled into balls, stuck on skewers and grilled; green peppers or zucchini stuffed with spicy ground lamb; and lamb burgers.

Today I buy local grass-fed lamb at farmer's markets. When local lamb is not available, I settle for New Zealand lamb.

Butterflied Leg of Lamb

I was introduced to grilled, butterflied leg of lamb in Switzerland. Rubbed with garlic and herbs, the lamb was grilled over embers of apple wood on a raised grate in the fireplace. My absolute favorite way with lamb.

1 leg of lamb, butterflied
4 cloves garlic, cut into flat slivers
1 cup dry red wine, more for the wine reduction
4 long sprigs rosemary, crushed
Pinch of salt
Salt and pepper

Several hours before grilling, or the night before, open the leg and insert slivers into skin and fatty parts of the lamb. (If the lamb has a thick layer of fat, I whittle it down to a thin one.)
Pour wine into baking dish large enough for the meat. Add the rosemary, salt and any leftover garlic. Turn leg over once in the wine and cover with foil.
Preheat outdoor grill.
Remove lamb from marinade and pat dry. Lightly rub salt over all surfaces and then repeat with ground pepper.
Sear each side for about 5 minutes over high heat.
Lower heat to medium and continue grilling each side for 15 minutes.
Remove from heat, cover with foil and let rest about 20 minutes.
While the meat is resting, pour the marinade plus another ½ cup of red wine, into a saucepan and bring to a boil. Reduce the heat and simmer to make a wine sauce reduction.
Remove rosemary and garlic bits before serving.
You'll have a dark colored sauce to pass around with the carved lamb.
Slice the meat to your preference.
This will yield everything from well done (the ends) to medium rare and pink (center).

8 to 10 servings

Half a leg works just as well if fewer servings are needed

Curried Lamb

One of my favorite lamb stews.

4 tablespoons vegetable oil
2 large onions, chopped
2 pounds lamb shoulder, cut into 1-inch cubes
3 tablespoons curry powder
1 tablespoon fresh ginger, grated
2 cloves garlic, minced
1 cup dry white wine
1 cup plain yogurt
Coconut flakes, toasted

In a Dutch oven heat 2 tablespoons oil. Add onion and sauté until softened. Remove with a slotted spoon.
Add remaining oil and brown the meat on all sides; do not crowd. Do it in two batches if necessary. Remove with slotted spoon.
Add curry and ginger and stir until fragrant, about 3-4 minutes. Add garlic and sauté for a minute.
Return onions and lamb to pot along with wine. Stir to blend all. Mix in yogurt, cover and simmer for 1 hour or until the meat is tender.
Sprinkle servings with coconut flakes.
Best served over basmati rice.

4 to 6 servings

Lamb with Dill Sauce

A nice change when lamb is served often.

4 tablespoons vegetable oil
1 cup scallions, chopped
2 large onions, chopped
3 pounds lamb shoulder, cut into 1-inch cubes
Salt and freshly ground pepper to taste
2 tablespoons fresh dill, minced
White wine as needed
½ teaspoon cornstarch mixed with
1 lemon, juiced

Heat oil in a Dutch oven to medium.
Add scallions and onions and sauté until barely soft. Push onions to the sides and add lamb. Sauté the meat, turning often until all sides changed color but not browned.
Add salt and pepper and barely cover the mixture with white wine. Bring to a simmer, add half of the dill, cover the pot and slowly simmer the lamb until done, approximately 1 hour.
Blend the cornstarch into to the lemon juice until smooth. Add to the lamb and simmer until the sauce is slightly thickened, stirring constantly.
Remove from heat.
Add the remaining dill. Taste, adjust seasonings and serve.

6 to 8 servings

Lamb and Onion Stew

The sauce goes really well with fluffy mashed potatoes.

1 small lamb shoulder, approximately 2 pounds
2 cups water, possibly more
⅛ teaspoon salt
1 bay leaf
1 tablespoon caraway seeds
5 onions, peeled and quartered
3 russet potatoes, peeled and halved
Freshly ground pepper

In a stew pot cover the lamb with water and bring to a boil. Add onions, salt, bay leaf and caraway seeds. Cover, lower the heat and simmer for 45 minutes.

Add potatoes and simmer for additional 45 minutes or until potatoes and onions are falling apart.

Remove the meat to a cutting board and let it cool.

Lift the potatoes out of the stew with a slotted spoon into a bowl, mash them and return them to the stew.

When the lamb is cooled, cut it into bite-size chunks and add them to the stew.

Add pepper and taste.

Serve hot.

4 to 6 servings

Roast Leg of Lamb

I use rosemary instead of mint for the sauce.

1 leg of lamb
Garlic cut into thin slivers
Salt
Rosemary springs
1 onion, cut into quarters
1 carrot, peeled, cut lengthwise and into 2-inch chunks
Gravy:
2 tablespoons all-purpose flour
Cold water
1 short fresh rosemary twig
Salt and pepper to taste

Preheat oven to 325°F. Have a roasting pan with a rack nearby.
If the lamb has a thick layer of fat, remove all but a thin layer with a sharp knife.
Make slits between fat and meat and insert garlic slivers on all sides of the meat. Rub the surface lightly with salt
Place wide-side up on the roasting rack. Scatter onions, carrots and rosemary under the rack.
Slide roasting pan into the middle part of the oven. Roast lamb 20 minutes per pound for very pink or 25 minutes per pound for more medium.
Remove from oven, put lamb on a platter and cover with foil to keep warm. Let the roast sit for at least 20 minutes.
Use this time for **making the sauce**, if desired.
Scrape all drippings and veggies into a saucepan. Heat over medium heat while stirring. Add 2 tablespoons flour and keep stirring for about 5 minutes to cook away the raw taste of flour.
Slowly add cold water (half water and half red wine if you like) while stirring and bring the sauce to simmer. Keep adding liquid until the gravy has the consistency of heavy cream.
Remove onions, carrots and rosemary twigs. Add fresh rosemary, salt and pepper and simmer for 10 minutes or more. Taste and adjust seasonings.
Carve the meat on a cutting board and arrange back on the platter. Pass gravy separately.
8 to 10 servings

Lamb Salad

All cooking is done a day ahead, ideal for a hostess to be with guests instead of cooking.

The recipe easily multiplies. I have prepared this for as many as 80 guests with attractive and tasty results.

2 pounds grilled leg of lamb
4 large tomatoes - cut into 8 wedges, grilled
2 large red peppers, cut in half, grilled and then into ¼-inch slices horizontally
2 large yellow peppers, same as above
2 large green peppers, same as above
2 large Vidalia onions, same as above
2 fennel bulbs, same as above
Oil for brushing vegetables when grilling
4 cups vinaigrette, recipe below

6 cups mixture of Radicchio, green and red leaf lettuce – torn into bite size pieces

Grill the lamb to medium. Set aside to cool.
Grill the vegetables, one variety at a time, setting aside to cool.
Combine lamb and vegetables in a large bowl. Pour 2 cups of vinaigrette over everything. Gently toss to blend.
Cover and refrigerate overnight.
Remove from refrigerator 1 hour before serving to take the chill off.
Arrange the mixed greens in a circle on a large platter.
Mound lamb and vegetables in the center.
Pass remaining vinaigrette in a dish to be spooned over servings.

6 to 8 servings

Vinaigrette for Lamb Salad

1 pint olive oil
1 cup lemon juice
½ cup dry red wine
8 shallots, minced
8 cloves garlic, minced
½ cup fresh basil, chopped
2 tablespoons spicy mustard
4 tablespoons fresh parsley, minced
¼ teaspoon salt
Freshly ground pepper to taste

Mix all ingredients well, if possible a few hours before using for flavors to develop.

Makes 1 quart

Lamb and Green Beans Stew

Lamb, green beans and savory are a different combination from the usual lamb stew.

1 pound lamb ribs or ½ lamb shoulder
1 onion
½ teaspoon salt, more to taste
1 quart water
3 russet potatoes, peeled and halved
1½ pounds fresh green beans, cut into 2-inch length
1 small bunch fresh summer savory, or 1 tablespoon dried
⅛ teaspoon freshly ground pepper
2 tablespoons fresh parsley, minced

Put lamb, onion, salt and water in a stewpot and bring to a boil. Cover, lower the heat and simmer for 1 hour.
Add the potatoes, simmer for 15 minutes.
Add savory, pepper and beans and simmer for another 30 minutes.
Remove ribs, onion, savory branches and potatoes, leaving any small savory pieces in the stew. Discard the onion.
Mash potatoes in a bowl and return to the pot.
Scrape meat off the ribs and return to the stew.
Bring it to a boil again, taste and serve in individual soup bowls. Sprinkle parsley over each serving.

4 servings

Pork and Veal

Currywurst	144
Pork Filet Surprise	145
Pork with Apples & Onions	146
Pork Shoulder Roast	147
Szegediner Goulash	148
Curried Veal Kidneys	149
Veal Blanquette	150
Osso Bucco	151

We never raised pigs in Vermont. But several of our friends did, so we were able to get excellent pork from them by trading. One cut-up and packaged lamb was traded for a quarter of a pig.

Pork used to turn out fairly dry after roasting because of the high internal temperature needed to be sure to eliminate trichinosis. Today, pork is considered done at lower temperatures, so the results are tender and moist. Much of the fat can be cut off giving delicious and less caloric servings.

Veal always was, and still is, extremely pricey. Nevertheless, I made it occasionally, especially when we had guests.

I often served Veal Blanquette at catered events.

Currywurst

Currywurst was invented in Berlin in 1949.

British soldiers stationed in the city gave ketchup, Worcestershire sauce and curry to a woman in the city. She created a spicy sauce to be drizzled over grilled pork or veal sausages.

Currywurst quickly became Berlin's favorite fast food. Snack bars all over the city have re-created the recipe. The aroma of grilled sausage and curry is in the air most hours of the day. Now it is world famous and even has its own museum since 2009.

While going to business school I had a part-time job making and serving Currywurst at a friend's parents Imbiss Stube – snack bar. I worked there weekends and at special events, where they had a concession.

There always was a crowd patiently waiting for their sausage.

Pork sausages – 1 per serving
Topping:
3 tablespoons ketchup
3 tablespoons Worcestershire
1 teaspoon vinegar
Freshly ground pepper
1 tablespoon curry
Additional curry powder for dusting

Mix the ingredients for the sauce and set aside. A large batch can be made and refrigerated.
The grilled or fried sausage gets several diagonal slashes across the top.
Cover sausage generously with the sauce and dust with curry from end to end.
Currywurst is served with a crunchy roll and French fries.

Pork Filet Surprise

A favorite do-ahead entrée.

1 sheet frozen puff pastry, thawed
1 pork filet, approximately 1 pound
2 tablespoons spicy mustard
Freshly ground pepper
1 egg, beaten with 1 tablespoon water

Preheat oven to 350°F. Cover a baking sheet with parchment paper.
On a lightly floured board roll out the pastry to be 1-inch wider on each end and 2½ times as deep as the filet.
Fold under the thin tapered ends of the meat. Spread the mustard on both sides of the meat. Center the filet on the dough. Pull the dough over the meat. Moisten the edges with the egg and pat together. Turn the package over to have it seam-side down.
Moisten the ends of the dough with egg and tuck underneath. Transfer to the baking sheet.
Brush the dough with the egg wash. Make about 10 slits through the dough to let out moisture during baking.
Bake 20 minutes. Cover pastry lightly with foil and bake an additional 20 minutes.
The filet can sit 20 to 30 minutes before serving, it retains the heat.
When serving cut into 1" slices.

3 servings

If more servings are needed, 2 filets easily fit on one baking sheet. Make sure to leave ample space between.

Pork with Apples and Onions

1 pork filet, approximately 1 pound, cut into three pieces
Salt and pepper
2 tablespoons unsalted butter
2 medium onions, cut into eights
2 apples, peeled, cored and cut into eights
½ cup dry white wine

Heat the butter over medium in a large frying pan. Rub the pork with salt and pepper. Brown the meat, approximately 5 minutes on each side.
Add the onions and apples around the sides of the pan and turn occasionally.
When the meat is brown, lower the heat and cook for an additional 10 to 15 minutes, turning it a couple of times.
When the apples are lightly browned, remove them to a platter and keep warm.
The pork is done when juice runs barely pink. Remove the meat and keep warm.
When onions are light brown and are beginning to fall apart, add them to the reserved apples.
Pour the wine into the pan and simmer for a few minutes.
Add onions and apples back into the pan to reheat.
Place filet chunks on 3 serving plates.
Divide the apple and onion mixture and scatter on top of and in front of the meat.
Drizzle the pan sauce over each.

3 servings

Pork Shoulder Roast

Pork shoulder is a special treat to serve a crowd. People seldom cook it at home because you can't really make it just for 2 or 4.
The skin makes 'crackling,' a very sought after tasty and crisp crust, cut into bite size morsels.

1 pork shoulder with skin – approximately 8 to 12 pounds
Salt and pepper

Preheat oven to 350^0.

With a sharp knife or razor blade, cut a diamond pattern all over into the skin.
Rub the meat with salt and pepper and put onto a rack in a roasting pan.
Roast 35 minutes per pound for a whole shoulder. Let the roast sit for at least 15 minutes.
Before carving, remove the crispy crust and break it into small pieces. Carve or pull the shoulder into small pieces. The meat will be tender and juicy.
Ideal for a casual buffet dinner.

A whole shoulder easily serves 20 or more.

Roast the smaller pork shoulder or butt for a smaller crowd.

Szegediner Goulash

A friend from Hungary gave me this, her mother's, recipe in exchange for my beef rouladen. We were both working in Switzerland and reminiscing about foods we missed.

I love this pork and sauerkraut combination, friends and family do as well.

Our bachelor friend George, once casually asked, "What are you cooking this time?" when I invited him. After dinner he told me, "I have to confess that I tried to find excuses why I couldn't come. I hate Sauerkraut! I had it almost every day as a kid. But this was delicious!"

2 tablespoons vegetable oil
2 pounds pork shoulder, cut into 1-inch cubes
2 32-ounce jars Sauerkraut, rinsed twice and drained
⅓ cup Hungarian paprika
2 large onions, chopped
1 cup white or red wine
1 cup sour cream
Salt and pepper to taste

In a large Dutch oven heat the oil over medium heat. Brown the pork without crowding, in batches if needed.
Cover meat with sauerkraut, stir well, cover and heat through, approximately 5 minutes. Add paprika and onions, stir until blended. Add the wine, cover tightly, turn heat to low and simmer approximately 2 hours or until meat is done. Add more liquid if needed.
When the meat is tender add sour cream, stir, cover and simmer 10 minutes.
Taste and adjust seasoning. Add additional paprika, salt and pepper if needed.

Serves 6 to 8

Curried Veal Kidneys

A dish I often made during our early, small food budget days. It is still delicious and special today.

1 tablespoon unsalted butter
1 tablespoon all-purpose flour
1 tablespoon curry
Pinch of salt
Cold water
1 slice pineapple, cut into small sections
¼ cup heavy cream

2 tablespoons slivered almonds

4 veal kidneys*, cleaned and tubes cut out and cut into thin slices
2 tablespoons unsalted butter
Salt and pepper

Heat the butter in a medium sauce pan. When foaming add curry, flour, salt and stir until mixture is roasted but not burnt. Slowly add the water while stirring, until the sauce is thickened to heavy cream consistency. Turn heat to low and simmer for 10 minutes. Add pineapple and cream, bring to a simmer again, cover and remove from heat.
Meanwhile toast the almonds in a frying pan until crisp but before they get brown. Set aside.
In a frying pan large enough to hold kidneys, heat the butter. Add kidney slices and quickly brown on all sides, dust with a pinch of salt and pepper.
Scrape browned kidney slices and all juices into the curry sauce. Add the almonds and blend well.
Reheat the sauce gently. Taste and adjust seasonings.
As soon as the mixture is starting to simmer, it is ready to be served.

4 servings

(* Beef kidneys also work well. Since they are larger, 2 will be sufficient.)

Veal Blanquette

Veal Blanquette is actually easy to prepare. Only the final minutes will require your complete attention. It was a popular dish at Ski Club 10 where lunch was served buffet style. I would finish small amounts at a time and always have fresh servings available for members.

2 pounds veal shoulder cut into 1-inch cubes
3 tablespoons unsalted butter
12 small white onions
2 tablespoons all-purpose flour
1 cup dry white wine
1 bay leaf, 1 sprig parsley
Salt and pepper to taste
3 carrots, sliced
½ pound white mushrooms, sliced
1 egg yolk mixed with
1 tablespoon lemon juice
1 cup heavy cream

Heat butter in a Dutch oven and sear the meat until light brown on all sides.
Add onions and brown lightly.
Add flour and stir for a few minutes but do not brown.
Add wine and bring mixture to a simmer while stirring. Add carrots, bay leaf, parsley, salt and pepper. Reduce heat, cover and simmer for 1 hour.
Add mushrooms and simmer for another 30 minutes.*
Remove pot from heat. While stirring add the yolks in a thin stream.
Add the cream and blend and return pot to stove. Stir while on very low heat. Mixture will thicken somewhat. Do not let it come to a boil or the sauce will curdle.
Serve immediately.

4 to 6 servings

(* The recipe can be prepared up to this point and refrigerated. About 1 hour before serving remove the pot from the refrigerator, letting the blanquette return to room temperature. Slowly heat it to a low simmer and continue with the recipe.)

Osso Bucco

I enjoyed Osso Bucco for the first time at a lakeside restaurant in Locarno, in the Italian region of Switzerland. It was delectable and is my personal favorite veal dish. But with the bone in the center of the cut contributing to the weight, the price is often prohibitive.

Veal shanks are rarely reduced. When I spot one, I quickly buy it. Driving home with my treasure I anticipate this succulent dish.

4 veal shanks
Salt and pepper
All-purpose flour for dredging
¼ cup coconut oil
1 small onion, diced
1 small carrot, diced
1 stalk celery, diced
3 Roma tomatoes, diced
2 large sprigs rosemary or 1 teaspoon dried
2 sage leaves or ¼ teaspoon powdered
1 cup mellow red wine
½ cup beef or veggie broth

Heat the oil over medium heat in a Dutch oven.
Mix flour for dredging with salt and pepper. Dry the shanks and dredge in the flour. Place them in the Dutch oven for browning. It may take 10 to 15 minutes to achieve the deep brown on each side. Remove the shanks and set aside.
Add onion, carrot and celery to the same pot and soften them slowly. Add more oil if needed. When vegetables are taking on color, add the tomatoes, stirring them into the mixture.
Add red wine and broth and bring to a simmer, stirring and scraping any bits and pieces off the bottom.
Add rosemary and sage and return veal shanks to the pot. Bring all to a slow boil. Reduce heat so that the sauce barely simmers. Cover the pot tightly and simmer for 1½ hours. Turn the meat over once after about 45 minutes.
When done the meat should fall off the bone and the sauce not too thin.
Serve over rice or polenta. Each serving includes the center bone with the delectable marrow.
4 servings

Wild Things

Bison Burger	153
Wild Duck	154
Dandelion Salad	156
Fiddlehead Fern Soup	156
Rabbit Ragout	157
Wild Mushroom Ragout	158
Baked Mushrooms	159
Venison Cobbler or Ragout	160

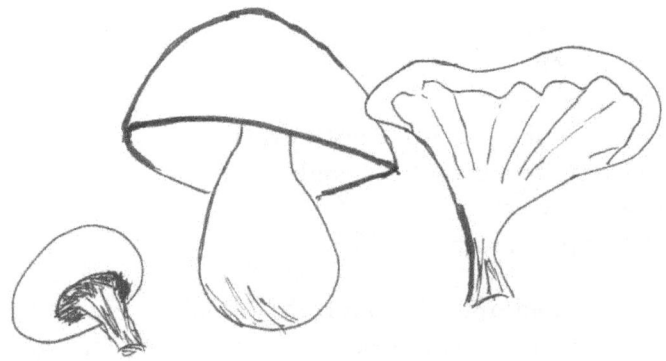

In Vermont, living many miles from town, surrounded by meadows and woods, had delicious benefits.

In the springtime young dandelions appeared in the grass right outside our kitchen door, a tasty addition to salads. Not long after, the first ferns started to grow on the side of roads and trails. Their emerging tops were shaped like the head of a fiddle and were turned into Fiddlehead Fern soup or a vegetable side dish. Every season brought new wild edibles.

In late summer and early fall, hunting season, Trent and Jason brought home mostly rabbits and deer.

We didn't catch all these wild things ourselves. Our friends also generously shared their bear, partridge and wild turkey with us.

Bison Burger

For excellent burgers you need freshly ground meat from a butcher. Bison, or buffalo, is not any different. The pre-packaged ground bison just does not give the same flavorful and juicy results.

I love to top the burger with hot jalapeño jelly or with caramelized onions, or both. See recipe page 65.

1 pound freshly ground bison
Salt
Freshly ground pepper
1 tablespoon vegetable oil
Jalapeño jelly as needed

You'll want to handle the meat as little as possible for best results. Divide meat into 3 equal parts. Carefully pry each pile open in the middle to expose the center. Lightly salt the meat and grind pepper into it. Lightly fold meat back over the center and flatten to about 1-inch thick. Salt both sides lightly and dredge in very coarsely ground pepper.
Let the meat sit for about 30 minutes.
In a heavy pan heat the oil and sear one side at medium heat for 4 minutes. Turn over with a spatula. Slightly press meat down so that as much of the meat as possible touches the pan. Sear again for 3 or 4 minutes.
Remove patties from heat, cover with foil and let rest for 5 minutes.

3 servings

I'm using ⅓ of a pound per person. Just buy more according to preference and servings needed.

Wild Duck

In the 1960s we received a windfall of wild ducks. Stein Eriksen left Sugarbush Ski Resort in Vermont, to be ski school director at Snowmass, Colorado. Our friend Rachel, who was Stein Eriksen's Ski School manager, coordinated moving. She came across six wild ducks in the freezer, remnants from one of Stein's duck hunting trips. "What shall we do with these?" she asked.

"Cook'm," he said.

Rachel brought the ducks to my kitchen. We called all the friends and bachelors that were in town for a feast the following evening. I roasted the ducks, braised red cabbage and made small potato dumplings. Others brought salad, bread, dessert and lots of wine. It was the ultimate pot-luck.

Preparation is similar to domestic duck or goose, but there are some differences.

1 Duck
4 to 6 bacon strips
Salt and pepper
2 apples, peeled and roughly diced
1 tablespoon cornstarch, blended with
1 cup giblet broth and red wine combination
Giblet broth, page 19 – keep liver separate
Duck liver, set aside

Red currant jelly

Preheat oven to 350^0.
Remove giblets and make a broth – page 19. Rub the duck with salt and pepper inside and out. Stuff the apples in the cavity and close it with toothpicks.
Wild duck isn't nearly as fatty as domestic fowl. Cover the breast and legs with the bacon strips to keep the meat from drying out.
Place duck on a rack on a roasting pan and slide it into the middle of the oven. Roast duck 15 minutes per pound – 10 minutes if you like the meat more red. Baste occasionally. When done, transfer the duck to a platter and keep warm.

Scrape bits and juices from the roasting pan into a sauce pan and reheat. In a small bowl combine cornstarch and the wine and giblet broth combination. Stir into the sauce pan and bring all to a simmer. When mixture has slightly thickened remove from heat and cover.

Sauté the liver in a small amount of butter a couple minutes on each side. Slice thinly and keep warm.

Remove the stuffing from the cavity. Carve the duck for serving.

Pass sauce, liver and stuffing separately.

Red currant jelly is a favorite accompaniment.

Wild duck is less meaty than domestic ones and yields 3 servings.

Dandelion Salad

Gather young leaves from emerging dandelions before flower buds appear.

Any area where you know that the ground has not been commercially fertilized is a safe place to pick. Early spring is the best time for harvesting these greens.

Dandelion leaves are good alone or in a mixed greens salad. Rinse well, dry and mix with your favorite dressing.

When looking along edges of rivers and streams you may also spot **wild watercress**. Go ahead, pick and enjoy in salads.

Fiddlehead Fern Soup

Fiddlehead fern season is very short. You can find them in forests, parks and at the edge of dirt roads. It is the early curled top – looking like a fiddlehead – you want to harvest. As soon as they start to uncurl and grow, they tend to taste bitter.

Cleaning can be time consuming, but they are a special seasonal treat.

1 quart fiddleheads, cleaned
1 can evaporated milk
2 veggie bouillon cubes
Salt and pepper to taste

Cook fiddleheads in a large pot of lightly salted water for 15 minutes or until tender. Drain, reserving the liquid.
Put fiddleheads in a blender with 2 cups of the reserved water, bouillon cubes, salt and pepper and blend well.
Add the milk. Add additional water if the soup is too thick.
Reheat the soup and serve.

3 to 4 servings

Instead of soup, fiddleheads can also be served as a vegetable.
A light sauté in unsalted butter, with a dash of salt and pepper, is all that's necessary.

Rabbit Ragout

1 rabbit, cut into serving pieces, thawed if frozen
Marinade:
2 cups dry red wine
1 cup sliced onions
½ teaspoon salt
½ teaspoon freshly ground pepper
4 cloves
1 bay leaf
1 teaspoon mild mustard

2 tablespoons vegetable oil
1 small onion, chopped
2 tablespoons pancetta or lean bacon, minced
2 tablespoons all-purpose flour
½ cup sour cream

Mix marinade in a glass bowl, add rabbit, making sure the meat is covered. Marinade for 24 hours or longer.
Remove meat and dry with paper towels. Heat oil in a Dutch oven, sauté bacon and onions until onions soften. Push to sides of the pot, add rabbit pieces and brown on all sides. Strain the marinade and pour over the rabbit. Bring to a boil. Cover, reduce heat to low and simmer for approximately 1 hour or until the meat is tender.
Remove rabbit to a platter and cover.
Put flour in a small bowl or cup and slowly add just enough water to make a smooth paste. Add to broth and let it come to a boil while stirring. Cook for a few minutes. Taste and adjust seasoning if needed. Add sour cream and stir until blended. Once the sauce reached the boiling point again, you are ready to serve.
Pour sauce over the rabbit.
Traditionally rabbit is served with noodles or potatoes.

3 to 4 servings

Wild Mushroom Ragout

My mother learned about mushrooming from her grandparents in the forests of Bohemia, now Poland. She visited us every summer in Vermont.

Together we went mushroom hunting. She showed us how to find chanterelles under fir trees. Boletus were more likely to grow in mossy and rocky areas. My mother made a point of not pulling mushrooms out of the soil, but cutting them at the base with a knife. By leaving the roots we assured new growth the following year.

Armed with knives and bags the family fanned out in all directions. Later we gathered and showed off our loot. On the way home we anticipated a delectable mushroom ragout dinner.

Chanterelles, Boletus and other easily recognized varieties can be spotted in most forests.

2 tablespoons unsalted butter, more if needed
¼-inch slice of Pancetta, chopped into small cubes
1 large onion, diced
1 pound chanterelle mushrooms*, cleaned and quartered
2 tablespoons all-purpose flour
1 cup broth or white wine or a combination
Salt & pepper to taste
3 tablespoons fresh parsley, chopped
2 tablespoons sour cream
1 tablespoon fresh parsley, chopped for garnish

Sauté Pancetta in melted butter until slightly browned over medium heat in a wide pan. Add onions and sauté until translucent. Add mushrooms, toss well until heated through, approximately 5 minutes. Dust mixture evenly with flour and mix until flour absorbed all moisture, add more butter if all seems too dry.

Add the liquid and gently stir until mixture starts bubbling. Add salt, pepper and 3 tablespoons parsley. Turn heat to low, cover and simmer for about 20 minutes.

Mix sour cream with a bit of the liquid from the ragout in a cup until smooth, add to ragout. Bring to a simmer again for about 5 minutes. Garnish with remaining parsley when serving.

4 servings
(*Any mushroom variety can be used instead.)

Baked Mushrooms

Mushroom hunting often brings abundance. Of course, you can sauté and freeze batches or dry and store them for future treats.
I do like to use them fresh and after I served mushroom ragout one night I make a batch of baked mushrooms the next day.

Large mushrooms, like Boletus, bring best results. The recipe works as well with Portobello's.

Measurements will vary since all depends on the amount of mushrooms you have.

1 egg, beaten with 1 tablespoon water
1 cup coarse breadcrumbs
¼ teaspoon salt
10 turns with the pepper mill
1 pound mushrooms, cleaned

Preheat oven to 350^0.
Line a baking sheet, or two, with parchment paper.
Slice mushrooms vertically from cap to the bottom of the stem starting in the middle of the cap. If caps are large, the end pieces will be without stem.
In a shallow, wide bowl add salt and pepper to the bread crumbs. Mix the egg with water in another shallow bowl. Have them side-by-side in your work area.
Dip mushroom pieces into the egg mixture and then into the bread crumbs. Be sure all areas are covered.
Place breaded mushrooms on a baking sheet. They can be close together but should not touch.
Slide baking sheet onto a rack in the middle of the oven and bake for 20 minutes.
Serve with a favorite dipping sauce or drizzle with olive oil.

Venison Cobbler or Ragout

When we were living in Vermont's Green Mountains, hunting was an annual fall ritual. After bringing home the trophy, it needed to be cut and packaged after a week or so.

This cobbler, a family favorite, was made with the scraps that accumulated in the process.

2 pounds venison*, cut into 1½-inch pieces, dusted with salt
2 tablespoons vegetable oil
2 large onions, diced
1 carrot, diced
1 stalk celery, diced
3 tablespoons all-purpose flour
1½ cups diced tomatoes
2 cups veggie broth
1 cup red wine
1 bay leaf, 5 juniper berries, salt and pepper to taste
1 pound white mushrooms, sliced
1 sheet frozen puff pastry
1 egg mixed with a little water

Heat the oil in a Dutch oven and brown venison. Remove.
Add onions, celery and carrots, lower heat to medium and sauté until onions soften lightly. Return meat and mix. Add the flour and stir until lightly browned. Add broth and bring to a low boil while stirring.
Add wine and bring to a boil again; sauce should be very thick. Add bay leaf, juniper berries, salt and pepper, cover and simmer over very low heat for 1 hour.
Add mushrooms and simmer for an additional 30 minutes. (Stop here if making ragout.) Dilute the sauce a bit with red wine and you'll have a tasty ragout to serve with noodles or rice.
Continue with cobbler: Defrost pastry. Preheat oven to 400°F.
Taste venison and adjust seasoning if needed. Remove bay leaf and juniper berries. Pour into a 9x12 ovenproof dish.
Roll out the pastry and stretch over the dish, about ½-inch down the sides. Make several cuts into the top of the pastry and brush with the egg mixture.
Bake for 30 minutes or until pastry is golden brown.
4 to 6 servings
(* Bear, elk or moose bring tasty results as well. Depending on the cut they may need additional cooking time.)

Finales

Almond Cake	163
Baked Alaska	164
Apple Cake	166
Cherry Cake	166
Plum Cake	166
Red Currant Cake	166
Rhubarb Cake	166
Apple Strudel	167
Black Forest Cake	168
Baked Apple	170
Carrot Cake	171
Cream Cheese Frosting	171
Cherry Clafouti	172
Cherry Sauce	172
Cream Puffs	173
Chocolate Éclairs	174
Decadent Chocolate Cake	175
Chocolate Rum Mousse	175
Holiday Truffles	176
Lemon Mousse	177
Raspberry Sauce	177
Meringues	178
Orange Delight	179
Peach Tart	180
Apple Tart	180
Plum Tart	180
Pickled Pumpkin	181
Plumped Fruit	182
Glühwein	182
Red Wine Sauce	183
Chocolaty Wine Sauce	183
Scones	184
Velvety Cheesecake	185

While growing up in Germany, desserts were served only on Sundays or on special occasions.

Raising our children in the States, we did the same. Seasonal fruit were the usual treats. It is also healthier not to top of a big meal with a rich dessert. Imagine the monumental job you are giving your digestive system! Sometimes we had ice cream or a piece of apple cake in the afternoon instead of after dinner.

Homemade vanilla ice cream, drizzled with our own maple syrup was always popular with our children. But when Ben & Jerry's in nearby Burlington started producing their silky smooth, high quality vanilla ice cream we stopped making our own at home.

A few years later Ben & Jerry's moved their facility to Waterbury Center, even closer and more convenient to us. I remember when they were selling "seconds" pints for 75 cents. Eventually Cherry Garcia, dotted with cherries and chocolate bits, became our family's favorite

Of course, dessert is always much anticipated at every special event. It doesn't have to be complicated, but it should be memorable.

Almond Cake

Almond cake always was on the buffet table at Ski Club 10. Members came back for second and more helpings. I learned quickly to make more cakes than one could possibly need so that almond cake always was available.

The cake can be dressed up by spreading a thin coat of chocolate glaze over the top, letting any excess drip decoratively over sides.

I like the simpler version, dusted with powdered sugar, best.

1 cup unsalted butter
1 cup sugar
1 cup almonds, skin on, ground
6 egg whites
¼ tsp vanilla
¼ cup all-purpose flour, plus flour for dusting the pan

Powdered sugar for dusting

Preheat oven to 375°F.
Coat a springform pan with butter and dust with flour.
Melt butter - just barely – in a large mixing bowl, add sugar and stir until creamy. First add almonds and blend. Then add one egg white at a time, fluffing them as they get incorporated. Finally blend in vanilla and then mix in the flour.
Pour into the prepared pan and bake about 45 minutes. Cool completely – dust with powdered sugar.

16 servings

Baked Alaska

It'll make a special occasion memorable and is worth the steps of getting it ready. Everything can be prepared ahead of time.
You just have to stand by the oven for the few minutes it takes for the meringue to be done and the Alaska is ready for serving.

1 pound cake, frozen and slightly defrosted
3 quarts of different ice cream flavors, i.e. 1 each of dark chocolate, pistachio and French vanilla, you'll have leftovers
6 egg whites beaten until stiff
⅛ teaspoon cream of tartar
½ cup sugar
Bottom round of a springform covered with parchment

When deciding on the ice cream flavors keep the finished product in mind. You'll want the outside layer to be dark to offset the light colored meringue.
Remove pound cake from package and thaw just enough so that it can be cut horizontally into ½-inch slices. Cover the spring-form bottom completely with the slices, pushing the cake tightly together, cut away any excess. Put in the freezer.
Use a stainless steel bowl, no wider than 8-inches by about 4 or 5-inches deep, for freezing the ice cream section. Soften ice cream, one flavor at a time. Spread a 1-inch layer of first flavor into the stainless steel bowl from the bottom all the way to the rim. Put into freezer until very firm, approximately 30 minutes.
Repeat with second flavor. Fill the remaining space completely with the third flavor.
When the ice cream is firm, dip the bowl into warm water. After a minute remove, quickly dry the outside with a towel and immediately turn the bowl upside down onto cake bottom letting the ice cream plop out. Cut the cake base to be even with the ice cream and transfer back to the freezer. Cover with plastic wrap once the ice cream is firm again and store until needed.
1 hour before serving prepare the Meringue. Beat egg whites and tartar until stiff. Slowly add sugar and continue beating until very stiff.

Remove ice cream cake from freezer. Quickly spread meringue over the ice cream and cake base as thick as possible. Make sure to seal all, including base. This will keep the oven heat from penetrating and melting the ice cream

The Alaska may be kept in the refrigerator for an hour or so at this point.

Preheat oven to 450°F.

When ready for dessert, quickly transfer the Alaska to the oven. Bake until meringue turns a light golden brown, about 5 minutes.

Remove from oven to a serving platter. If the springform bottom does not easily separate from the cake base, just leave it on.

Cut with a thin, strong knife, continually dipping the blade into very warm water.

8 to 12 servings

Apple Cake

A favorite in any season.

In order of preparation:

Blend in a large bowl:
¼ cup of vegetable oil
½ cup of sugar
⅛ teaspoon almond extract
1 egg
½ cup of milk and mix until smooth

Blend in a small bowl:
1½ cups of all-purpose flour
2 teaspoons baking powder
⅛ teaspoon salt

Topping:
3 or 4 Granny Smith apples, peeled, cut in half, remove core, cut into app ¼-inch slices.
Cinnamon, 2 tablespoons butter, 2 tablespoons sugar

Preheat oven to 375°F. Butter a spring form pan or rimmed baking sheet.

Add dry mix to the large bowl and blend just enough until all is moist – do not over mix.

Scrape cake mixture into prepared pan and spread evenly to sides – makes a rather thin layer if a baking sheet is used.

Arrange apple slices on top – standing on the inner edge – one slice next to the other, pushing onto dough for support. Start at the outer circle in springform pan - straight rows on baking sheet - and continue until all is covered.

Dust with cinnamon, dot evenly with slivers of butter and then sprinkle the sugar over the top.

Slide into the middle of the oven and bake approximately 20 to 30 minutes or until any visible dough is golden brown.

Let cool in pan. Serve with whipped cream.

8 to 12 servings

The same recipe can be used to make **Plum**, **Cherry**, **Rhubarb** or **Red Currant Cake** with slight changes.

If using cubed **rhubarb** or whole red **currents**, spread additional sugar on the top of these tart fruits.

For **plum** cake: remove the pits, cut plums into quarters and press skin side down into the dough. For **cherry** cake: cut cherries in half, remove the pit and press skin side down into the dough.

Apple Strudel
An often requested dessert.

It used to be difficult and time consuming when puff pastry had to be made from scratch. I gratefully use frozen puff pastry now.

1 sheet puff pastry, thawed
3 Golden Delicious apples - peeled, halved, cored, sections cut into ¼-inch slices
Juice ½ lemon
¼ cup sugar
1 teaspoon cinnamon
¼ cup currants
Rum to cover currants
¼ cup finely chopped almonds
2 tablespoons unsalted butter cut into thin slices
1 cup heavy cream, dash of vanilla, 1 teaspoon powdered sugar to make whipped cream
1 teaspoon powdered sugar to dust over top before serving

Preheat oven to 375°F.
Put currants into a small narrow bowl and cover with rum.
Cover a baking sheet with parchment paper.
Open puff pastry sheet, on lightly floured surface roll it out to 14x12 dimensions. Place on the baking sheet.
Toss apples in a bowl with lemon juice. Mix sugar and cinnamon well. Add to apples and toss. Add almonds and toss. Drain currants, add to the apples and mix well.
Pour onto lower third of the pastry sheet, the wider section of the rectangle, making a hill about 3-inch wide across leaving 1-inch on either end uncovered. Scatter butter all across.
Carefully pull far end of pastry toward you and over apple mixture and tuck underneath, moisten all edges with water. Press pastry ends together and fold under. Make 1-inch wide cuts into top in regular intervals all the way through the pastry to let out steam while baking.
Bake approximately 25 to 30 minutes until golden brown. If pastry gets dark too soon, cover lightly with foil.
Dust entire strudel with powdered sugar. After the pastry has cooled, cut into 1-inch serving pieces.
Serve with whipped cream.

12 servings

Black Forest Cake

This was my children's birthday cake of choice.

Always looking for shortcuts, I chose a devil's food cake mix and found it worked perfectly as a support for whipped cream and cherries. I usually skipped the traditional Kirsch liqueur, it is delicious as is.

1 box devil's food cake
1 14-ounce jar of Bing cherries, drained – 12 cherries set aside
6 tablespoons red currant jelly
2 tablespoons unflavored powdered gelatin
6 tablespoons milk
4 cups heavy cream
1 teaspoon vanilla extract
6 tablespoons powdered sugar
Dark chocolate to make shavings

Bake cake according to directions in a cake round or springform pan. Cool completely.
Meanwhile sprinkle gelatin over the milk in a small bowl. Let sit to dissolve.
Pour cream and vanilla into a bowl large enough to accommodate the finished whipped cream. Whip on medium for a few minutes until is starting to thicken. Add dissolved gelatin and 2 tablespoons sugar. Continue on medium. Every time sugar has been absorbed add more sugar while whipping until all sugar has been worked in. Set speed to high and whip until the cream has reached the desired triple volume.
With a potato peeler make thin shavings off a block of dark chocolate, enough to be the final touch on top of the cake. Set aside

Assembly:
Cut cake horizontally into three even layers.
Place one layer on a serving platter, and spread 3 tablespoons of jelly evenly over the round. Take ⅓ of the whipped cream, spread half of it on top of jelly. Distribute all but the reserved 12 cherries across the round and top with the remainder half of the ⅓ of whipped cream.
Center the second layer on top and gently press down. Spread remainder of jelly evenly over the layer and top with another ⅓ of whipped cream.
Top with the remaining cake round, pressing in place gently. Scrape any cream, emerging from the layers around the side of the cake.
Spread remaining whipped cream across the top and sides.
Space the reserved cherries evenly around the top's outer rim.
Pile the chocolate shavings in the center.
Chill at least 2 hours, up to 6, in the refrigerator to allow the frosting to get firm.

Cut the cake into 12 even slices with a clean, sharp knife.

12 servings

This is one recipe where I use sugar, but I make sure it is organic.

Fancy Baked Apples

The aroma of baking apples transports me back to my childhood in Berlin every time.

As soon as my mother opened our apartment door in the winter, the scent of apples and cinnamon escaped into the cold stairwell. I knew immediately that whole apples were baking in the Ofenröhre (The metal insert in a tile oven that was the heat source in the living room during the long winters). The 12x12-inches insert stayed hot while the coals burned. Mother usually kept tea warm in the insert.

We poked the apples frequently for doneness while they were baking. When they were finally done, I'd bite into the soft sweet-tart flesh, savoring taste and warmth.

This recipe is a bit fancier version.

1 sheet puff pastry, thawed
4 Golden Delicious apples, peeled and cored
½ cup walnuts, chopped
4 teaspoons maple syrup
2 tablespoons unsalted butter, cut into 4 chunks
1 teaspoon prated lemon peel
½ teaspoon cinnamon
Pinch of nutmeg
1 egg yolk beaten with teaspoon cold water
Heavy cream as needed

Preheat oven to 400°F.
Cut puff pastry into 4 6-inch rounds. Place each on top of every other muffin pan hole, pushing the pastry into the hole ever so lightly.
Fill the apple cavity with nuts, pour a teaspoon of maple syrup over it, dust with lemon peel, cinnamon and a scant pinch nutmeg and top it all off with a ½ tablespoon butter.
Put an apple into the center of each pastry. Pull pastry close to the apple, bending it outwards at the top. Brush all visible pastry with the egg yolk.
Bake on the bottom shelf of the oven for 10 minutes. Lower heat to 375°F and bake an additional 25 to 30 minutes, or until the apples are golden brown.
Serve warm with a bit of heavy cream poured over the apple.

Carrot Cake

Be sure to use young, sweet carrots for the best results.

1 cup vegetable oil
½ cup sugar
2 teaspoons maple syrup
2 teaspoons vanilla extract
4 eggs
1 cup all-purpose flour
1 cup whole wheat flour
2 teaspoons cinnamon
2 teaspoons baking soda
⅛ teaspoon salt
2 cups carrots, grated
1 8-ounce can crushed pineapple, drained, reserve 2 tablespoons juice
¾ cup walnuts, chopped
1 cup shaved coconut

Preheat oven to 350^0 F. Grease a 9x13 baking pan.
By hand or with a mixer combine first 5 ingredients. In a separate dish mix flours, soda, cinnamon and salt and blend into mass in a large bowl. Add carrots, pineapple and juice, walnuts and coconut. Mix well, pour into prepared pan and distribute evenly with a spatula.
Bake for 45 minutes in the middle of the oven.
Frost after it cooled and cut into squares.

12 servings

Cream Cheese Frosting

¾ cup cream cheese, softened
2 tablespoons unsalted butter, softened
1 teaspoon vanilla
2 tablespoons milk
¼ cup powdered sugar

Blend cream cheese, butter and vanilla to a smooth consistency, and then add the milk. Gradually blend in the sugar.
Spread over the cake after it cooled.
The frosting makes a good topping for other cakes as well.

Cherry Clafouti

A dessert classic that can also be made with apples, blueberries, pears or plums.*

2 pounds cherries, pits removed
⅓ cup sugar
4 eggs
¾ cup all-purpose flour
¼ cup heavy cream
1 teaspoon vanilla extract
Pinch of salt

Preheat oven to 350°F. Butter a baking dish or pie pan.
Spread cherries over bottom of dish.
Mix eggs and sugar until smooth. Gradually mix in the flour, slowly add cream, vanilla and salt while whisking and pour over the cherries. Bake for 45 minutes to 1 hour until lightly browned. Serve hot.

6 to 8 servings

(* Peel and cut apples and pears into small slices; cut plums in half; use blueberries whole.)

Cherry Sauce

Topping for ice cream, meringues or crepes.
This topping is as popular as it is versatile. If it is handy, the sauce can even be a last-minute addition to the pan of sautéed duck breast. Just reheat the cherries while mingling with pan juices and serve.

2 cups dry red wine
¼ cup red currant jelly
2 cups frozen cherries – I prefer Bing cherries
2 tablespoons orange rind
Thaw cherries in a bowl, drain and reserve the liquid
In a medium sauce pan heat the wine and simmer until down to 1 cup and the consistency is slightly syrupy – about 30 minutes.
Add jelly and orange rind. Bring to a simmer again.
Add cherries and reserved juice, bring to a boil and simmer for a couple of a minute. Remove from heat and let cool.

Remove orange rind before serving or storing in the refrigerator.

Cream Puffs

Besides anything chocolate, this is my all-time favorite dessert.

¾ cup water
6 tablespoons unsalted butter, cut into pieces
⅛ teaspoon salt
¾ cup all-purpose flour
3 eggs
1 cup heavy cream
⅛ teaspoon vanilla extract
2 teaspoons powdered sugar, some more for dusting

Preheat oven to 425°F, line a baking sheet with parchment paper,
In a saucepan combine water, butter and salt and bring to a boil over medium heat. When the butter is dissolved add the flour while stirring. Continue stirring until the mixture is forming a ball, pulling away from the sides of the pan. Remove pan from the heat and let the mixture cool off for about 5 minutes.
Add the eggs to the cooled mixture, one at a time, continually beating. The mixture will separate briefly each time an egg is added but will get smooth again with beating.
Transfer the batter into a pastry bag (or a Ziploc bag with a ½-inch cut off one corner) and pipe dough into rounds 2-inch in diameter and 1-inch high onto the baking sheet, leaving spaces between each.
Bake until puffed and golden brown, about 20 to 25 minutes. Take baking sheet from oven. Pierce the bottom of each pastry with a fork and place back on the baking sheet. Return them to the oven. Prop the oven door open while the pastries crisp for 3 minutes.
Let them cool completely on a rack.
While they are cooling, combine heavy cream and vanilla and whip until it starts to puff up. Add the sugar while whipping and continue until the cream is very stiff.
Cut each pastry in half and place a huge dollop of whipped cream in the center. Top with the other half and dust generously with powdered sugar.

12 servings

Chocolate Éclairs

This delectable treat uses the same recipe as Cream Puffs with slight variations. The dough is shaped oblong, filled with pastry cream and a chocolate glaze is the final touch.

Pastry cream:
1 cup milk
½ cup sugar
2 tablespoons cornstarch
½ teaspoon vanilla extract
2 egg yolks
1 tablespoon unsalted butter
Pinch of salt

Combine first five ingredients in a sauce pan. Bring the mixture to a simmer over very low heat, stirring constantly. Remove from heat when it begins to thicken. Stir in butter and salt.
Pour mixture into a bowl, cover with plastic wrap and let it cool. Refrigerate until needed.

Chocolate glaze:
¼ cup heavy cream
4 ounces semi-sweet chocolate, broken into pieces
Heat cream in sauce pan and melt. Keep at room temperature.

Assembly:
When the cream puff dough is ready, pipe it into oblong cigar like shapes, leaving space between each.
Proceed to bake like cream puffs.
When cooled off completely, cut éclairs in half horizontally. Spread pastry cream onto bottom half and replace the top. Spread chocolate glaze thinly on top.

12 servings

Decadent Chocolate Cake

So easy and so good.

1 pound bittersweet chocolate
10 tablespoons unsalted butter
1 tablespoon unbleached all-purpose flour
1 tablespoon sugar
4 eggs, separated
1 cup heavy cream

Preheat oven to 425°F. Line the bottom of a springform pan with parchment paper.
In the top of a double boiler melt the chocolate slowly. Remove the bowl from heat and stir in butter, sugar and flour.
Beat the egg whites until they are firm but not stiff. Fold egg whites quickly into the lightly cooled chocolate mixture.
Pour mixture immediately into the springform and bake for 15 minutes. Turn off the heat and open the oven door, leaving it ajar by propping a wooden spoon in the door. Let cake cool completely.
Meanwhile whip and flavor the heavy cream to your liking.
Cut cake into thin portions with a sharp knife and serve with a generous dollop of whipped cream.

12 servings

Chocolate Rum Mousse

1½ cups half and half
5 egg yolks
1½ cups semi-sweet chocolate chips
A pinch of salt
3 tablespoons dark rum
Whipped cream for serving

Scald cream in a saucepan over medium heat. Set aside to cool slightly.
Put egg yolk, chocolate chips, salt and rum in a blender. Pour the warm cream in a steady stream into the mass while processing.
When smooth pour the mixture into a bowl. Cover with plastic wrap and refrigerate for at least 4 hours, or until the mousse is firm.
Scoop onto desert plates and top with whipped cream.
4 servings

Holiday Truffles
They are popular any time of the year.

¼ cup heavy cream
2 tablespoons rum, or Grand Marnier or Kahlua
6 ounces bittersweet Belgian chocolate, broken into small pieces
4 tablespoons unsalted butter, softened
Powdered cocoa

In a small saucepan boil the cream until it is reduced to 2 tablespoons. Add rum and chocolate and melt over low heat while stirring.
Whisk in the softened butter until smooth. Pour mixture into a shallow dish and refrigerate until firm.
Ready a plate with cocoa powder. With a teaspoon scoop truffle mixture from bowl, form into small balls and roll in the cocoa.
Keep truffles in a covered container in the refrigerator, serve at room temperature.

24 truffles

The recipe can be multiplied many times with the same results.

Dipped Truffles
When I make a large batch of truffles I dip some of them in melted chocolate.

You'll need:
Toothpicks, foam board and white and dark chocolate.

Melt chocolate in separate small bowls over a double boiler. Stick a toothpick into a truffle and dip into chocolate. Quickly remove, letting any excess drip back into pot.
Stick the toothpick into foam board and proceed with the next one.
When hardened, remove toothpick and place each in a decorative candy paper cup.

Lemon Mousse

At our son Derek's wedding eve party I served Lamb Salad. Lemon Mousse was the perfect light and delicious dessert to follow.

I love the flavor combination of lemon and raspberries,

1 envelope unflavored gelatin
¼ cup water
4 eggs, separated
¾ cup sugar
2 lemons, juiced
Grated peel from one ½ lemon
Salt, pinch

In a small bowl sprinkle gelatin over cold water.
Beat egg yolks in bowl of double boiler, add 2/3 cup sugar and blend.
Stir over hot water until thickened, approximately 10 minutes.
Remove from heat, add gelatin and mix to dissolve. Add lemon juice and grated peel. Set aside to cool.
In a bowl add salt to egg whites and beat until almost done. Gradually add remaining sugar, continue beating until shiny. (An electric hand mixer is the best tool for this.)
Fold egg whites into the cooled lemon mixture. Transfer to a 4 cup bowl.
Refrigerate at least 4 hours.
Serve with raspberry sauce – recipe below.

6 servings

Raspberry Sauce

1 10-ounce package frozen red raspberries
1 tablespoon cornstarch
Defrost berries and reserve ½ cup of their juice.

In a small saucepan blend cornstarch and 2 tablespoons of juice. Add remaining juice.
Stir over low heat until clear and thickened.
Remove from heat, add berries and adjust taste for sweetness.
Chill and serve with separately with desert.
Both recipes are easily multiplied.

Meringues

Versatile meringue recipes adapt to your need. You can make small meringue kisses, or a large base to hold fruit.

3 egg whites
½ teaspoon cream of tartar
⅛ teaspoon salt
¾ cup white sugar

Preheat the oven to 250°F. Line two baking sheets with parchment paper.
Beat the egg whites, cream of tartar and salt, by hand or with an electric mixer, to the soft peaks stage.
Slowly add the sugar, 2 tablespoons at a time, until the mixture is stiff and glossy.
Put 4 mounds of meringue on each baking sheet. Form each mound into a 3-inch round. Make an indent in the middle of each, to hold future fillings.**
Bake on the lower and middle shelf of oven for 1 hour and 45 minutes. Change location of baking sheets half-way through baking.
Move baking sheets to racks and let cool completely.

8 servings

(** Skip the indent if meringues are to be used like cookies. Or, pipe small mounds onto baking sheet to make meringue kisses. Shorten baking time for the small ones.)

The center of the meringue can be filled with any fruit combination.

The recipe can easily be doubled.

Orange Delight

The recipe is based on one by James Beard that was featured in a magazine. He came across this dessert at a small country inn outside of Cannes, France.

It is a light dessert with great visual impact.

6 Valencia oranges, all the same size
1 pint orange sherbet – more if oranges are large
Meringue topping:
3 egg whites, cold
A pinch of salt
⅛ teaspoon cream of tartar
6 tablespoons sugar

Cut tops off oranges one-third down, hollow out – reserving the orange pulp for a fruit salad or juicing.
Place oranges upside down on a small baking sheet and freeze.
Soften sherbet and fill oranges to the top and return to freezer until frozen solid.*
When ready to serve, preheat oven to 450^0 F.
Beat egg whites with salt and cream of tartar until they hold soft peaks. (An electric hand mixer works best.) While beating slowly, add sugar and continue beating until mixture is stiff and shiny.
Take the baking sheet with the oranges from the freezer. Divide the meringue into 6 portions and pile onto oranges, spreading the mixture all the way to the edges.
Bake for 5 minutes or until meringue is light brown.
Serve immediately.

6 servings

(* Can be prepared up to one week ahead to this point.)

Lazy Days Peach Tart
A summer favorite.

Crust:
1 cup all-purpose flour
Grated peel from 1 orange
⅛ teaspoon salt
8 tablespoons unsalted butter, chilled – cut into small pieces
3½ tablespoons water
1½ teaspoons orange juice

Filling:
5 medium peaches
2 tablespoons rum or brandy
2 teaspoons sugar
¼ teaspoon cinnamon
⅛ teaspoon allspice, ground
2 tablespoons unsalted butter

Combine flour, orange peel, salt and butter in food processor and pulse. When mixture resembles cornmeal add water and juice, process until dough begins to stick together. Remove dough and shape into a disk. Cover with plastic wrap and refrigerate for at least 30 minutes or until ready to use.
Preheat oven to 425°F.
Slice peaches into ¼" sections, toss with rum.
On a floured board roll dough into an approximately 13-inch round. Transfer onto a baking sheet.
Starting 2-inches from the edge, cover the dough with circles of peach slices. Dot with butter, sprinkle with sugar, cinnamon and allspice. Pull uncovered dough over the filling, pinching excess dough into folds.
Bake for 15 minutes, then reduce to 375°F and continue baking until pastry is lightly browned.
When cooled serve with slightly sweetened whipped cream or ice cream.

8 servings

Use the same recipe for an **Apple** or **Plum Tart.**

Grandmother's Pickled Pumpkin

Sometimes, when I couldn't find anything to do, I went to my grandmother's kitchen. She was always cooking something. I watched as she prepared eel, tripe, lung, brain and other, to me, revolting foods. They reminded her of childhood in the country where during slaughtering nothing was wasted.

But in the fall, her kitchen often was filled with the sweet-tart smell of pickled pumpkins. I couldn't wait for the cooking to be finished to sample some while still hot, as grandmother was filling glass jars with the pieces. Those were good, but they were even better cold. She loved making them. Grandmother gave many of those filled jars as presents.

One way to use up a bumper crop of pumpkins

5 cups diced pumpkin, approximately 1-inch cubes
2 cups water
2 cups cider vinegar
¼ cup distilled vinegar
½ cup maple syrup or sugar
1 teaspoon whole cloves
1 large cinnamon stick

Place diced pumpkin in a large non-metallic bowl. Combine remaining ingredients in a saucepan and bring to a boil. Pour liquid over pumpkin and make sure all pieces are submerged. Cover the bowl tightly and set aside. After 8 hours, or so, strain the liquid and boil for 5 minutes. Add pumpkin and boil for an additional 5 minutes or until pumpkin is transparent but still crisp.

Cool the mixture and store in the refrigerator.

Plumped Fruit
A Christmas Eve tradition.

1½ pounds mixed dried fruit
Water
1 pint heavy cream
1 teaspoon powdered sugar
¼ teaspoon vanilla extract
Cinnamon for dusting

At least two days before serving:
Put fruit in a medium bowl – higher rather than wide. Cover with water and let stand. Check once in a while to make sure no fruit is floating.
With a mixer or by hand, whip cream. When it is starting to get fluffy add vanilla and powdered sugar, continue beating until there are firm peaks.
Serve fruit with a generous dollop of whipped cream and dust lightly with cinnamon.

8 servings

Glühwein

Another must - not only at Christmas time, but throughout the holiday season. Who can resist when the aroma of wine, fruit and spices permeates the air? Even as a child, I always had a small glass of Glühwein. Its tradition!

6 cups water
1 cup sugar
2 cinnamon sticks
30 cloves
6 bottles mellow red wine
1 lemon, juiced
1 orange, juiced and zest thinly julienned

Heat first four ingredients in a pot large enough to hold the finished Glühwein. Stir occasionally until sugar is completely dissolved.
Remove from heat, add wine, lemon, orange and blend all. Reheat, but do not boil. Keep warm throughout serving time.
30 to 40 servings

Red Wine Sauce

Serve cold over rice pudding or ice cream as an alternative to chocolate sauce. I always have some in the refrigerator, just in case – one never knows. I have even served it with a less flavorful grilled steak. It worked.

1 cup mellow red wine
1 cup water
¼ cup sugar
1 clove
A pinch cinnamon
2 tablespoons cornstarch

Combine wine, water, sugar, clove and cinnamon and slowly bring the mixture to a boil. Let it simmer, uncovered, for 5 minutes.
Mix cornstarch with a little water to a paste. Add it to the wine mixture bring it to a boil again while stirring. Remove from the heat immediately once it reached the boiling point.
It is easy to make in a larger quantity and refrigerate. ring to room temperature before serving.

Chocolaty Wine Sauce

Use if for dipping fruit, pour over ice cream or pound cake.

¼ cup cream
6 ounces semi-sweet chocolate, broken into chunks
1 tablespoon unsalted butter, room temperature
½ cup red wine sauce – above recipe

Heat the cream in a sauce pan, add the chocolate and let it melt slowly.
Blend in the butter and then add the red wine sauce. Gently stir and blend.
Serve warm.

Makes 1 cup

The recipe is easy to prepare in larger quantities.

Crumbly Scones

If I'm having company and looking for something to have with an afternoon cup of tea, it most often is a scone. Scones should be light and almost fall apart when tearing off a piece to slather with fresh butter and raspberry jam.

The best scones are to be found all over the British Isles. I enjoyed a perfect one in the heart of London and keep that in mind when I'm getting ready to make a batch.

2 cups all-purpose flour
2 teaspoons baking powder
1 teaspoon sugar
¼ teaspoon salt
1 teaspoon grated lemon zest
8 tablespoons unsalted butter, at room temperature
2 eggs
½ cup cream or milk
¾ cup currants (optional)

Preheat oven to 450º.
In a mixing bowl combine the first five ingredients.
With a pastry cutter mix in the butter.
Reserve a little egg white. Beat the rest and combine with the milk. Add the mixture to the bowl along with currants – if used. Mix all gently. Gentle, is important. The dough should just be firm enough to handle.
Put dough on a floured board. Knead just enough until the dough holds together, about 1 minute.
Pat the dough into an oblong shape, 3/4-inch thick. Cut into even diamond shapes or use a cookie cutter for round scones.
Mix the reserved egg white with a 1 teaspoon water and brush over the top.
Bake 15 minutes.
Serve warm.

Makes about 15 scones.

Velvety Cheesecake

A no-bake cheesecake that's keeping the kitchen cool on sultry summer days.

    Cheesecake was a staple on the dessert table at Ski Club 10. One time I was trying another cake in its place and faced many disappointed patrons. If I ever experimented with another dessert again, it was always in addition to cheesecake and almond cake, the other 'must have'.

1 Graham cracker pie crust, baked or bought
2 8-ounce packages cream cheese, room temperature
1 small packet vanilla instant pudding
1½ cups milk
1 teaspoon vanilla extract

Have 9-inch pie crust ready to be filled.
By hand blend ½ cup of milk and cream cheese until smooth. Add remaining milk and vanilla and blend. Add pudding mix and immediately stir rigorously until smooth and pour at once into pie crust. Spread the mixture evenly to the edges. Chill for several hours.

12 servings

Serve plain <u>or</u> with cut fresh fruit <u>or</u> with slightly sweetened whipped cream.

OR

Add the following topping after mixture is set and firm:

¾ cup sour cream
½ cup powdered sugar
2 Tb butter, softened
1 tsp vanilla

With an electric hand-mixer cream together sour cream, butter and vanilla. Add sugar and mix until smooth. Spread evenly over the cheesecake.

Refrigerate the cake until serving.

Edible Flowers

You'll want to be sure that the flowers you choose are organic if they are meant to be stuffed, added to salads or the final, edible decorative touch of a dish.

Blossoms from your own garden or another equally reliable source are best.

A
Apple Blossoms
B
Bachelor Buttons
C
Carnation
Columbine
Chrysanthemum
Clover
D
Day Lily (not Lily of the Valley),
Dandelions
E
Elderberry blossoms and berries
English Daisy
F
Fuchsia blossoms and berries
G
Gardenia
Gladiola
H
Herbs' flowers
Hibiscus
Hollyhock
I
Impatients
J
Jasmine
Lavender
K
L
Lilac
M
Mallow,
Marigold
N
Nasturtium - leaves as well as flowers,
Nigella
O
P
Pansy,
Passion flower,
Petunia,
Peony
Poppy seeds for baking
Q
Queen Anne's Lace
R
Roses
S
Scented Geranium,
Snapdragon,
Sunflower
Sweet Woodruff
T
Tulip
V
Violet,
Verbena
W
Wax Begonia
Y
Yucca petals
Z
Zucchini Blossoms

Index

A
About Potatoes, 73
About Wines, 4
Almond Cake, 163
Apple Cake, 166
Apple Strudel, 167
Apple Tart, 180
Artichoke Appetizer, 7

B
Bacon Sauce, 30
Baked Alaska, 164
Baked Apple, 170
Baked Fennel, 69
Baked Mushrooms, 159
Baked Whole Tomatoes, 65
Basic Broth, 20
Basil and Garlic Pasta, 53
Beef and Beer, 120
Beef Ragout Country Style, 119
Beef Salad, 121
Beef Short Ribs, 124
Belgian Endive Salad, 58
Bison Burger, 153
Black Bean Soup, 21
Black Forest Cake, 168
Black Forest Chowder, 22
Boiled Eggs, 94
Braised Cuts, 124
Brown Sauce, 29
Butterflied Leg of Lamb, 135

C
Caramelized Onions, 65
Carrot Cake, 171
Celery Root Salad, 58
Ceviche, 101
Cherry Cake, 166
Cherry Clafouti, 172
Cherry Sauce, 172
Chicken Cacciatore, 107
Chicken Flambé, 108
Chicken Liver Pâté, 8
Chicken Paprika, 109
Chicken Salad Tarragon, 110
Chocolate Éclair, 174
Chocolate Rum Mousse, 175
Chocolaty Wine Sauce, 183
Coq au Vin, 106

Country Style Tomato Soup, 23
Cream Puffs, 173
Creamed Onions, 66
Creamed Spinach, 67
Crêpes, 45
    Stacked Crêpes Dinner, 46
    Savory, 46
    Dessert, 46
Cream Cheese Frosting, 171
Crumbly Scones, 184
Crusty Italian Loaf, 36
Cucumber Salad, 59
Curried Lamb, 136
Curried Veal Kidneys, 149
Curried Veggie Stew, 68
Currywurst, 144

D
Dandelion Salad, 156
Decadent Chocolate Cake, 175
Dessert Crepes, 46
Deviled Eggs, 9
Dipping Sauce, 14
Duck Breast, 111

E
Easy Shrimp, 101
Edible Flowers, 186
Egg Basics, 94
    Boiled Eggs, 94
    Fried Eggs, 95
    Poached Eggs, 94
    Scrambled Eggs, 95
Egg Drop Soup, 20
Egg Salad, 97
Eggs in Mustard Sauce, 96
Escargot, 10
European Rolls, 40

F
Fancy Brussels Sprouts, 69
Farro Salad, 78
Favorite Goose, 112
Fiddlehead Fern Soup, 156
Fillet of Sole, 102
Five-Spice Chicken, 113
Focaccia, 37
French Bread, 39
French Onion Soup, 24
Fresh Pasta, 52
Fried Eggs, 95

G

Garlic Butter, 10
Garlic Bread, 40
Garlic Mashed Potatoes, 73
Glühwein, 182
Ginger Dressing, 121
Gravy De-mystified, 28
Green Beans á la Provence, 70
Grilled Chicken, 114
Grilled Veggie Dinner, 71
Guacamole, 11
Grouper, 103

H

Herb Dip, 18
Herbed Puff Pastry Rings, 12
Hockey Chili, 125
Holiday Truffles, 176
Hungarian Goulash, 126

I

Irish Soda Bread, 38
Italian Rosemary Bread, 41
Italian Sub, 44

K

Kale, 87
Kohlrabi, 72
Kohlrouladen, 128
Königsberger Klopse, 122

L

Lamb in a Blanket, 13
Lamb and Onion Stew, 138
Lamb with Dill Sauce, 137
Lamb Salad, 140
Lamb & Green Beans, 142
Lamb Shanks, 124
Leg of Lamb Roast, 139
Lemon Mousse, 177
Lentil Soup, 25
Liver- Berlin Style, 127

M

Manicotti, 53
Mashed Potatoes, 73
Meat Loaf, 130
Mayonnaise, 25
Meringues, 178
Millet, 79
Mock Hollandaise, 31
Mostaccioli, 54
Mustard Pickles, 82
Mustard Sauce, 96

N

New Potatoes, 74
Navajo Fry Bread, 47
Navajo Taco, 47

O

Oatmeal Bread, 38
Onion Marmalade, 92
Orange Delight, 179
Osso Bucco, 151
Oven Roasted Chicken, 115
Oven Roasted Veggies, 86
Oxtail Ragout, 124

P

Pasta, 52
Pasta with Basil and Garlic, 53
Pasta Carbonara, 55
Peach Tart, 180
Pesto Sauce, 30
Pickled Pumpkin, 181
Pizza, 49
    Basic, 49
    Thin Crust, 50
    Toppings, 49, 51
Plum Cake, 166
Plumped Fruit, 182
Plum Tart, 180
Poached Eggs, 94
Polenta, 80
Pork Filet Surprise, 145
Pork with Apples & Onions, 146
Pork Shoulder Roast, 147
Pot Roast, 131
Pot Stickers, 14
Potato Dumplings, 75
Potato Pancakes, 76
Potato Salad, 77
Poulet Flambé, 108
Presto Pasta, 56
Pumpkin Seed Pate, 15

Q

Quick Tomato Sauce, 32
Quiche, 98
    Leek, 98
    Spinach and Onion, 99
Quinoa, 79

R

Rabbit Ragout, 157
Ratatouille, 83
Raspberry Sauce, 177

Raw Snacks, 15
    Cocoa Bliss Balls, 15
    Apricot Bliss Balls, 15
    Sunny Spread, 15
Raw Tomato Sauce, 32
Red Cabbage, 84
Red Currant Cake, 166
Red Wine Sauce, 183
Rhubarb Cake, 166
Roasted Chicken, 115
Roasted Garlic, 85
Roast Leg of Lamb, 139
Roasted Veggies, 86
Rouladen, 132
Rye Bread, 42

S
Salad Dressing, 60
Salsa, 11
Sandwiches, 43
Sauerkraut, 88
Sauerkraut Salad, 61
Savoy Cabbage, 88
Scrambled Eggs, 95
Scones, 184
Snapper Blues, 104
Sopa de Ajo, 26
Spaghetti Sauce, 33
Spanish Rice, 133
Spicy Carrot Soup, 27
Spinach and Rice, 89
Spring Greens Salad, 61
Stacked Crepes, 46
Steak Tartar, 16
Steamed Mussels, 17

Stuffed Cabbage, 128
Stuffed Mushrooms, 18
Stuffed Tomatoes, 67
Sweet Potatoes, 89
Szegediner Goulash, 148

T
Tabbouleh, 81
Thai Chicken, 116
Tomatoes Provencal, 90
Tomato Platter, 62
Tomato Salad, 62
Turkey Gravy, 29

U
Upside-down Quiche, 98

V
Veal Blanquette, 150
Veggie Chili, 126
Velvety Cheesecake, 185
Venison Cobbler, 160
Venison Ragout, 160
Vinaigrette, 60, 141

W
White Sauce, 28
Whole Wheat Bread, 44
Wild Duck, 154
Wild Mushroom Ragout, 158
Wild Rice, 91
Wilted Salad Greens, 99
Winter Broth, 20

Y
Yogurt Sauce, 113

Z
Zucchini with Dill, 92

My Essentials Tools

In the early 1970s a good friend gave me her complete 20-piece stainless steel *Revere* set when she switched to a smooth glass cooktop. The pots and pans are 1930s vintage with heavy copper bottoms. Included in the set are an 8-quart stock pot; a 14-inch frying pan with lid that comes in handy for blanching vegetables and cooking whole asparagus; a double boiler and more. The pots are my prized possession, I use them every day.
Following is additional equipment that I use constantly.

Baking stone – Not just for pizza baking. My 14x14-inch stone stays in the oven, keeping temperatures even.

Cast Iron Frying Pans – 6 and 12-inch, seasoned. Cast iron has the best heat distribution. They are in daily use.

Dutch Oven – I have a 6-quart orange enameled Le Creuset one. It is the only pot I use for slow cooking stews and braises.
It is reliable for holding an even temperature.

Electric Hand Mixer - For whipping egg whites and cream.

Garlic Press – When I need the finest mince possible, I crush the cloves in the press. The garlic dissolves while cooking, leaving the flavor only.

Graters - With fine and regular options – fine for parmesan cheese and onions; regular for other cheeses and potatoes. I find it easier to reach for a grater than to turn on the Cuisinart. The hand grater also makes a finer mass.

Immersion Blender - Perfect for pureeing soups and sauces directly in their pots; less clean-up too.

Kitchen Scale – A metric scale is indispensable for recipes –especially bread recipes – with metric measurements.

Knives - I have several for boning meat, chopping veggies, slicing bread, etc. But, I couldn't do without a small one, with a 4-inch serrated blade; I even use it for stirring.

Raw Snacks, 15
    Cocoa Bliss Balls, 15
    Apricot Bliss Balls, 15
    Sunny Spread, 15
Raw Tomato Sauce, 32
Red Cabbage, 84
Red Currant Cake, 166
Red Wine Sauce, 183
Rhubarb Cake, 166
Roasted Chicken, 115
Roasted Garlic, 85
Roast Leg of Lamb, 139
Roasted Veggies, 86
Rouladen, 132
Rye Bread, 42

S
Salad Dressing, 60
Salsa, 11
Sandwiches, 43
Sauerkraut, 88
Sauerkraut Salad, 61
Savoy Cabbage, 88
Scrambled Eggs, 95
Scones, 184
Snapper Blues, 104
Sopa de Ajo, 26
Spaghetti Sauce, 33
Spanish Rice, 133
Spicy Carrot Soup, 27
Spinach and Rice, 89
Spring Greens Salad, 61
Stacked Crepes, 46
Steak Tartar, 16
Steamed Mussels, 17

Stuffed Cabbage, 128
Stuffed Mushrooms, 18
Stuffed Tomatoes, 67
Sweet Potatoes, 89
Szegediner Goulash, 148

T
Tabbouleh, 81
Thai Chicken, 116
Tomatoes Provencal, 90
Tomato Platter, 62
Tomato Salad, 62
Turkey Gravy, 29

U
Upside-down Quiche, 98

V
Veal Blanquette, 150
Veggie Chili, 126
Velvety Cheesecake, 185
Venison Cobbler, 160
Venison Ragout, 160
Vinaigrette, 60, 141

W
White Sauce, 28
Whole Wheat Bread, 44
Wild Duck, 154
Wild Mushroom Ragout, 158
Wild Rice, 91
Wilted Salad Greens, 99
Winter Broth, 20

Y
Yogurt Sauce, 113

Z
Zucchini with Dill, 92

My Essentials Tools

In the early 1970s a good friend gave me her complete 20-piece stainless steel *Revere* set when she switched to a smooth glass cooktop. The pots and pans are 1930s vintage with heavy copper bottoms. Included in the set are an 8-quart stock pot; a 14-inch frying pan with lid that comes in handy for blanching vegetables and cooking whole asparagus; a double boiler and more. The pots are my prized possession, I use them every day.
Following is additional equipment that I use constantly.

Baking stone – Not just for pizza baking. My 14x14-inch stone stays in the oven, keeping temperatures even.

Cast Iron Frying Pans – 6 and 12-inch, seasoned. Cast iron has the best heat distribution. They are in daily use.

Dutch Oven – I have a 6-quart orange enameled Le Creuset one. It is the only pot I use for slow cooking stews and braises.
It is reliable for holding an even temperature.

Electric Hand Mixer - For whipping egg whites and cream.

Garlic Press – When I need the finest mince possible, I crush the cloves in the press. The garlic dissolves while cooking, leaving the flavor only.

Graters - With fine and regular options – fine for parmesan cheese and onions; regular for other cheeses and potatoes. I find it easier to reach for a grater than to turn on the Cuisinart. The hand grater also makes a finer mass.

Immersion Blender - Perfect for pureeing soups and sauces directly in their pots; less clean-up too.

Kitchen Scale – A metric scale is indispensable for recipes –especially bread recipes – with metric measurements.

Knives - I have several for boning meat, chopping veggies, slicing bread, etc. But, I couldn't do without a small one, with a 4-inch serrated blade; I even use it for stirring.

Nutmeg Grater - Freshly ground nutmeg has more intense flavor.

Pizza Peel – For pizza and bread baking.

Pepper Grinder – I never buy ground pepper, only peppercorns. Freshly ground pepper packs the most punch.

Potato Ricer – For the lightest, fluffiest mashed potatoes.

Poultry Shears –I usually by whole chickens and poultry shears make dissecting a whole bird a cinch. To me, shears are easier to handle than heavy knives.

Pressure Cooker – I prefer one over a microwave, keeping electronic rays out of the house.

Rolling Pin – Not only for pastry and dough. The rolling pin is handy for cracking peppercorns between sheets of plastic wrap when I need them very coarse. I also prefer coarse bread crumbs over the powdery variety. I make them by placing day-old bread slices between dishtowels and crushing them with the rolling pin.

Slotted Spoons – Stainless steel spoons with long handles, some with small holes and others with large slits are perfect for lifting gnocchi or vegetables out of the cooking water, or removing sautéed meats from a pan without the fat.

Springform Pan – For cakes and breads. The removable bottom makes it a cinch to get the cake onto the cooling rack.

Wooden Cutting Boards - For making breads and pasta, prepping meat, and more. They are movable and easier to clean than an entire kitchen counter or table top.

Most 'Dog Eared' Cookbooks

A French Chef Cooks At Home by Jacques Pepin
Simon & Schuster, 1980
I identified with Pepin's no-nonsense approach to cooking and respect for food with the publication of his first cookbook in 1975. I went to one of his cooking demos at Macy's basement in New York in the 1980s. He is as genuine as his books.

Bouquet de France by Samuel Chamberlin
An Epicurean Tour of the French Provinces
Gourmet, 1952
and
Italian Bouquet by Samuel Chamberlin
An Epicurean Tour of Italy
Gourmet, 1958
Both books are travelogues by region with recipes in the copy. Sometimes it took me a minute to realize that I was reading a recipe. Published in the 1950s and still good reading.

Art Of Simple French Cookery by Alexander Watt
Rasher Verlag, 1961
These French bistro recipes are as promised: simple! Some of my favorite foods are rooted here.

Fanny Farmer Cookbook
Little, Brown and Company, 1870 – revised often
When in doubt, check with Fanny Farmer. The answers to your questions are there.

Greene on Greens by Bert Greene
Workman Publishing, 1984
and
The Grains Cookbook by Bert Greene
Workman Publishing, 1988
Bert Greene zeroed in on greens and grains, two much neglected food categories in the 1980s. He demonstrated their versatility, especially that of grains. The recipes are timeless.

How To Eat Better For Less Money by James Beard
Simon and Schuster, 1954
All the less expensive cuts of the 1950s and 1960s demand gourmet prices now. Beef bones were free. Kidneys were 25 cents a pound; lamb shanks, ox-tails and short ribs were about the same. Today I'm looking for deals on those, often after a major holiday when I'll stock up.

James Beard's Menus For Entertaining by James Beard
Delacorte Press, 1965
I relied on this book heavily whenever I planned formal meals.

Italian Family Cookbook by Edward Giobbi
Vintage Books, 1978
It was my turn-to cookbook when making fresh pasta became part of my cooking arsenal. It was an introduction to the variety of Italian recipes. I liked the focus of meal planning for the family.

Mastering The Art Of French Cooking
by Julia Child, Louisette Bertholle & Simone Beck
Alfred A. Knopf, 1961
I always loved Julia Child's enthusiasm. But, the first thing I did was to take her recipes apart, to devise short cuts. I was already familiar with the basics she was describing. Imagine, changing Julia Child's recipes! Of course, this was before she became JULIA CHILD.

New York Times Cookbook Edited by Craig Clairborne
Harper & Row, 1961
When I was attempting a new recipe early in my career, I referenced several cookbooks: James Beard's, Julia Child's and this one. Then I settled on the one that appealed to me the most. Sometimes it turned into a combination of several recipes.

Practically Macrobiotic by Keith Michell
Thornsons Publishing Group, 1987
This book was an eye-opener into the world of alternate diets. The recipes are simple and delicious and I still use many of them today.

The French Pocket Cookbook by Ginette Mathiot
Pocket Books, 1965
This translation of a French cookbook was the first cookbook I bought after Trent and I got married in 1965. I paid all of 50 cents for it. It holds many recipes with brief descriptions. No baking or roasting temperatures, just slow, medium or hot oven. When I was looking for ideas to cook something different, that's the book I turned to.

The Silver Palate Cookbook
by Julee Rosso & Sheila Lukens
Workman Publishing, 1978
A fun cookbook to read. Many reprints later, the recipes and attitude towards good food are as fresh today as when the book was first published.

Uncle John's Original Bread Book by John Rahn Braue
Pyramid Books, 1969
Baking bread at home was not widely practiced in the 1960s. I was eager to learn all about baking when I came across this little paperback. All the basics from sourdough to gluten-free are included. It became my bread bible. This was way before focaccia became popular.

New favorites are: Mark Bittman*, Melissa Clark and David Tanis, all are cookbook authors with regular columns in the New York Times.

I like **Mark Bittman's** approach to food. He's getting the most out of ingredients with the least possible effort.
Same goes for **Melissa Clark**. Her recipes are about food, not showmanship.
David Tanis champions simple recipes, fresh ingredients and a sense of adventure in the kitchen.
Sam Sifton, New York Times food editor, has a weekly 'no fuss food' column that I regularly read and get inspired.

*Mark Bittman no longer has a column.

About the Author

Heidi Smith lives in Taos, New Mexico,
with husband Trent.

The author will make presentations to groups.
It can be a cooking demonstration
or
a Question and Answer discussion.

Contact her via the website:
www.HeidiSmithGroup.com

or by email:
smithheidim@gmail.com

Credits

Cover and interior sketches by the author.

All photographs are the property of the author.

www.ingramcontent.com/pod-product-compliance
Lightning Source LLC
Chambersburg PA
CBHW022128080426
42734CB00006B/271